Houghton
Mifflin
Harcourt

CALIFORNIA

M A T H

Expressions
Common Core

Dr. Karen C. Fuson

GRADE

2

Volume 2

This material is based upon work supported by the
National Science Foundation
under Grant Numbers
ESI-9816320, REC-9806020, and RED-935373.

Any opinions, findings, and conclusions, or recommendations expressed in this material
are those of the author and do not necessarily reflect the views of the National Science Foundation.

Printed in the U.S.A.

ISBN: 978-0-544-21079-0

14 15 16   0868   23 22 21

4500819724   B C D E F G

VOLUME 2 CONTENTS

UNIT 4 Subtract 2-Digit Numbers

BIG IDEA 1   Totals of Mixed Coins and Bills

BIG IDEA 2   Multidigit Subtraction Strategies

* This lesson consists only of activities from the Teacher Edition.

VOLUME 2 CONTENTS **iii**

VOLUME 2 CONTENTS *(continued)*

UNIT 5 Time, Graphs, and Word Problems

VOLUME 2 CONTENTS *(continued)*

UNIT 7 Arrays, Equal Shares, and Adding or Subtracting Lengths

* This lesson consists only of activities from the Teacher Edition.

© Houghton Mifflin Harcourt Publishing Company

Student Resources

Family Letter

Content Overview

Dear Family:

In this unit, your child will find the value of various coin combinations. Children will also combine different coins to equal one dollar.

$$25¢ + 25¢ + 10¢ + 10¢ + 10¢ + 10¢ + 10¢ = 100¢$$

Then your child will count both dollars and coins.

Say: $1.00 $1.25 $1.35 $1.40

You can help at home by providing opportunities for your child to practice counting money. Begin with amounts less than $1.00.

Please call if you have any questions or concerns. Thank you for helping your child to learn mathematics.

Sincerely,
Your child's teacher

© Houghton Mifflin Harcourt Publishing Company

CA CC

Unit 4 addresses the following standards from the *Common Core State Standards for Mathematics with California Additions*: **2.OA.1, 2.OA.2, 2.NBT.4, 2.NBT.5, 2.NBT.6, 2.NBT.7, 2.NBT.7.1, 2.NBT.8, 2.NBT.9, 2.MD.8,** and all Mathematical Practices.

Carta a la familia

Un vistazo general al contenido

Estimada familia:

En esta unidad su niño va a hallar el valor de diversas combinaciones de monedas. Los niños también combinarán diferentes monedas para igualar el valor de un dólar.

25¢ + 25¢ + 10¢ + 10¢ + 10¢ + 10¢ + 10¢ = 100¢

Luego, su niño contará billetes de dólares y monedas.

Se dice: $1.00 $1.25 $1.35 $1.40

Usted puede ayudar a su niño proporcionándole en casa oportunidades de practicar contando dinero. Empiece con cantidades menores que $1.00.

Si tiene alguna duda o algún comentario, por favor comuníquese conmigo. Gracias por ayudar a su niño a aprender matemáticas.

Atentamente,
El maestro de su niño

© Houghton Mifflin Harcourt Publishing Company

CA CC

En la Unidad 4 se aplican los siguientes estándares auxiliares, contenidos en los *Estándares estatales comunes de matemáticas con adiciones para California*: **2.OA.1, 2.OA.2, 2.NBT.4, 2.NBT.5, 2.NBT.6, 2.NBT.7, 2.NBT.7.1, 2.NBT.8, 2.NBT.9, 2.MD.8** y todos los de prácticas matemáticas.

Explore Quarters

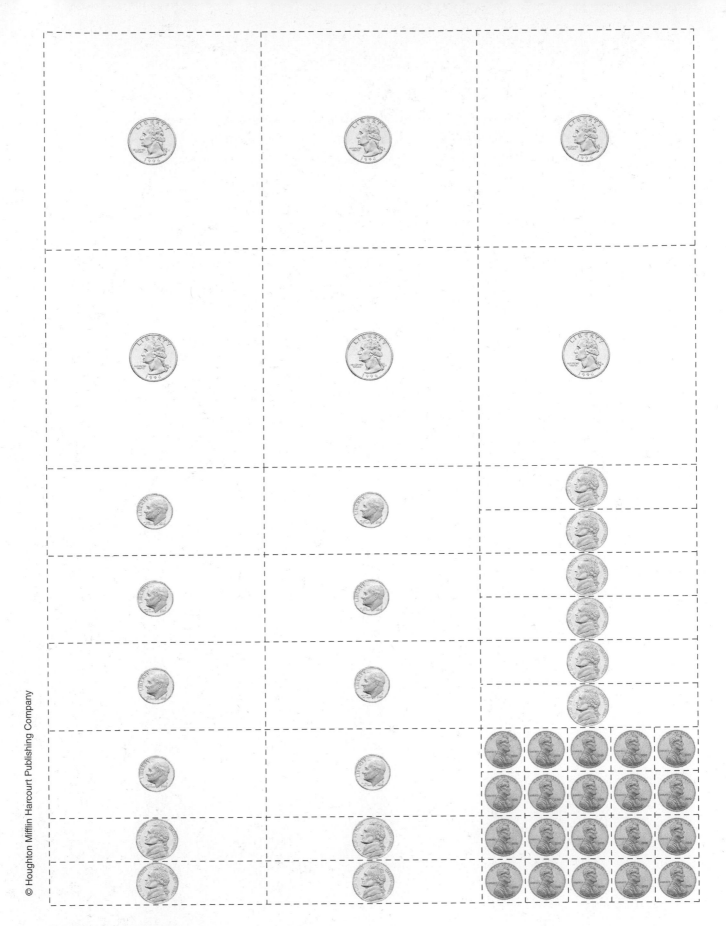

Cut on dashed lines.

© Houghton Mifflin Harcourt Publishing Company

Coin Cards

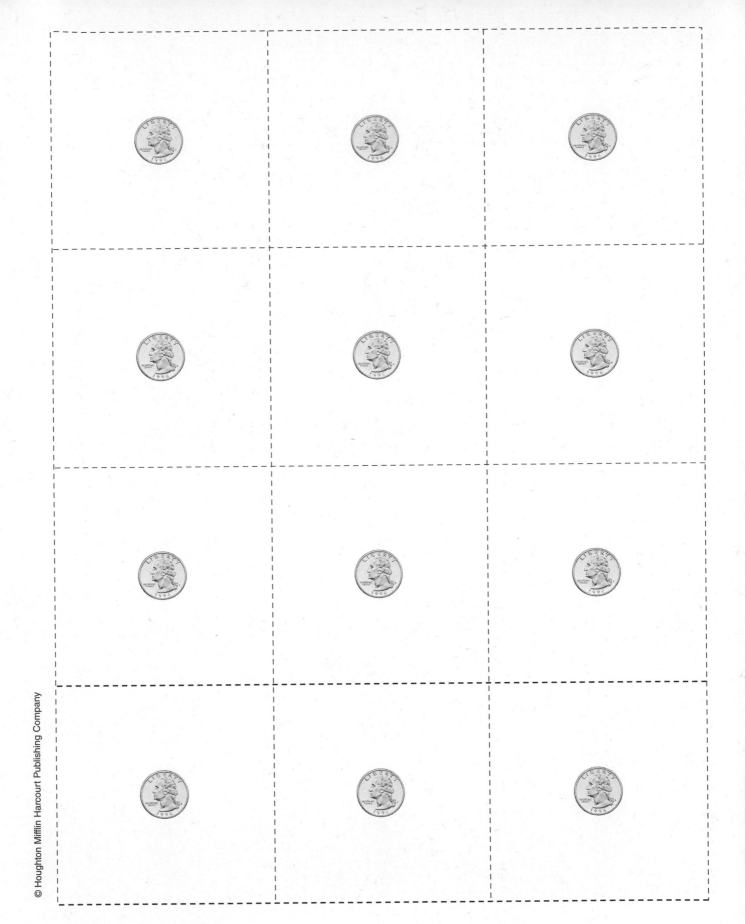

Cut on dashed lines.

© Houghton Mifflin Harcourt Publishing Company

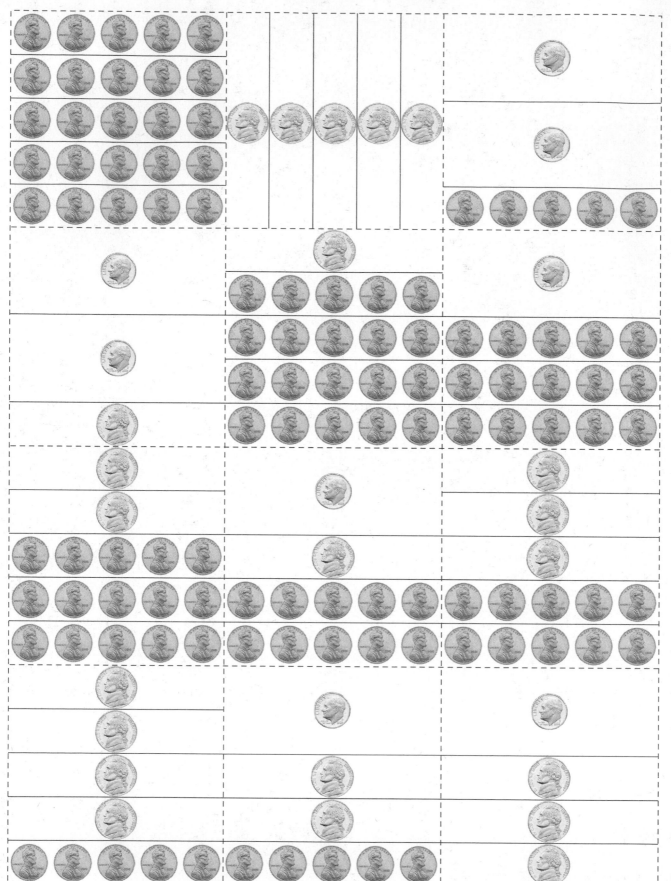

Cut only on dashed lines.

Quarter Squares (back)

Cut on dashed lines.

Dollar Equivalents (front) **165**

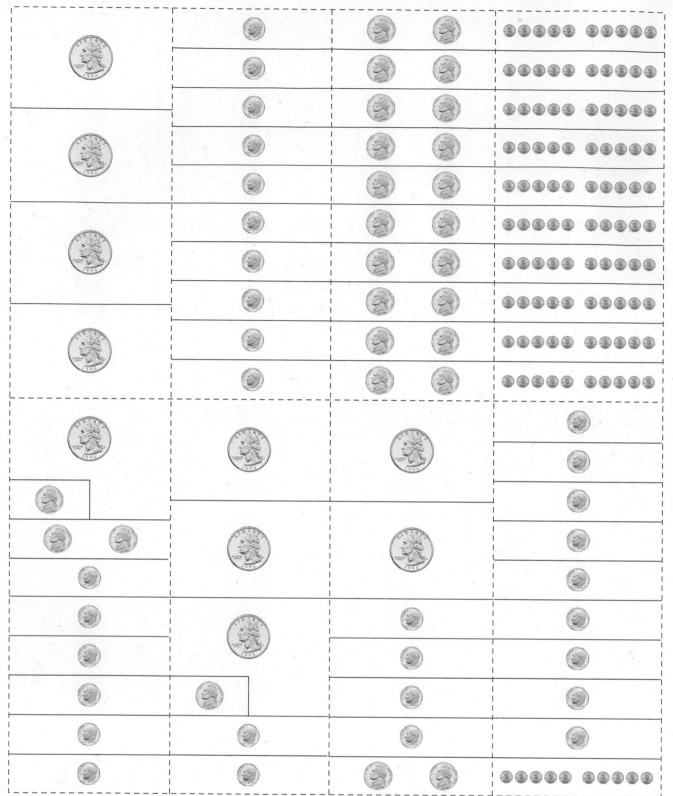

Cut only on dashed lines.

Dollar Equivalents (back)

► Count Coins and Bills

Under each picture, write the total amount of money so far.
Then write the total using $. The first one is done for you.

1.   25¢   25¢   10¢   5¢

25¢   50¢   60¢   65¢ $ <u>0</u> . <u>6</u> <u>5</u>
                                            total

2.   25¢   10¢   10¢   1¢   1¢

___ ___ ___ ___ ___ $ ___ . ___
                                       total

3.   100¢   25¢   5¢   5¢

___   ___ ___ ___ $ ___ . ___
                                       total

4. Bo has 1 dollar, 2 quarters, 1 dime, 4 nickels, and 3 pennies.
Draw ☐100 s, (25) s, (10) s, (5) s, and (1) s.

Write the total amount of money. $ ___ . ___
                                                total

▶ What's the Error?

100¢   1¢   1¢

$ _1_ . _2_ ___

I wrote the total. Did I make a mistake?

5. Show Puzzled Penguin how you would find the total amount of money. Under each picture, write the total amount so far.

100¢   1¢   1¢

_____   _____   _____ $ ___.___ ___
                                             total

▶ More Practice Writing Totals

Under each picture, write the total amount of money so far.
Then write the total using $.

6.   100¢   5¢

_____   _____ $ ___.___ ___
                                             total

7.   100¢   5¢   1¢   1¢

_____   _____   _____ _____ $ ___.___ ___
                                                  total

Explore Dollars

4-3 Class Activity

Name ____________________

CA CC Content Standards 2.OA.1, 2.NBT.1a, 2.NBT.5, 2.NBT.7, 2.NBT.9 Mathematical Practices MP.1, MP.4

VOCABULARY
ungroup

► Word Problems: Ungrouping 100

When you subtract, you can use the following drawings to help you **ungroup**.

Use Dollars to Ungroup	Use Quick Tens to Ungroup
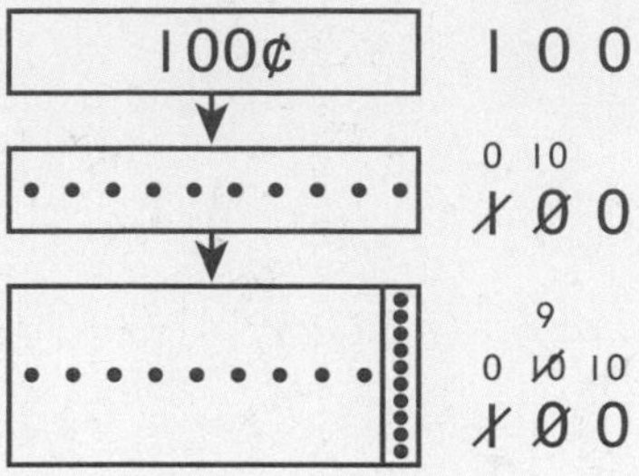	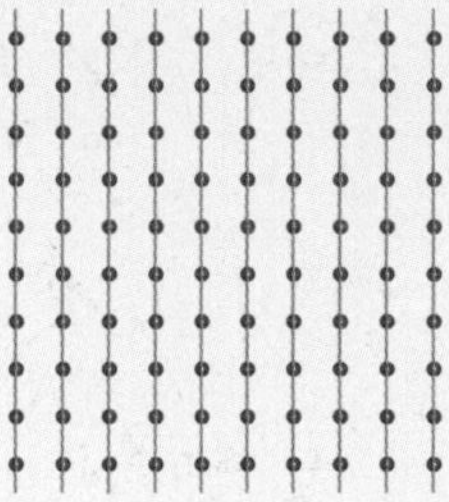

Solve the word problems. **Show your work.**

1. The baker bakes 100 loaves of bread. He sells 73 loaves. How many loaves are left?

   ☐ ____________________
   label

2. Jim has 100 flowers in his garden. He gives 35 of them away. How many flowers are left in Jim's garden?

   ☐ ____________________
   label

3. The letter carrier has 100 letters in her bag. She delivers 52 letters. How many letters are left in her bag?

   ☐ ____________________
   label

► Subtract from 100

Solve. Rewrite the hundred or make a drawing.

4. $100 - 62 = \boxed{}$

5. $100 - 83 = \boxed{}$

6. $100 - 79 = \boxed{}$

7. $100 - 54 = \boxed{}$

Addends and Subtraction

Family Letter

Content Overview

Dear Family:

In this program, children learn these two methods for 2-digit subtraction. However, children may use any method that they understand, can explain, and can do fairly quickly.

Expanded Method	Ungroup First Method
Step 1 "Expand" each number to show that it is made up of tens and ones.	**Step 1** Check to see if there are enough ones to subtract from. If not, ungroup by opening up one of the 6 tens in 64 to be 10 ones. 4 ones plus these new 10 ones make 14 ones. We draw a magnifying glass around the top number to help children focus on the regrouping.

$$64 = 60 + 4$$
$$-28 = 20 + 8$$

Step 2 Check to see if there are enough ones to subtract from. If not, ungroup a ten into 10 ones and add it to the existing ones.

$$64 = \overset{50}{\cancel{60}} + \overset{14}{\cancel{4}}$$
$$-28 = 20 + 8$$

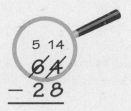

Step 2 Subtract to find the answer. Children may subtract from left to right or from right to left.

Step 3 Subtract to find the answer. Children may subtract from left to right or from right to left.

$$64 = \overset{50}{\cancel{60}} + \overset{14}{\cancel{4}}$$
$$-28 = 20 + 8$$
$$\overline{30 + 6 = 36}$$

In explaining any method they use, children are expected to use "tens and ones" language. This shows that they understand they are subtracting 2 tens from 5 tens (not 2 from 5) and 8 ones from 14 ones.

Please call if you have any questions or comments.

Sincerely,
Your child's teacher

 CA CC

Unit 4 addresses the following standards from the *Common Core State Standards for Mathematics with California Additions*: **2.OA.1, 2.OA.2, 2.NBT.4, 2.NBT.5, 2.NBT.6, 2.NBT.7, 2.NBT.7.1, 2.NBT.8, 2.NBT.9, 2.MD.8,** and all Mathematical Practices.

Estimada familia:

En este programa, los niños aprenden estos dos métodos para restar con números de 2 dígitos. Sin embargo, pueden usar cualquier método que comprendan, puedan explicar y puedan hacer relativamente rápido.

Método extendido	**Método de desagrupar primero**
Paso 1 "Extender" cada número para mostrar que consta de decenas y unidades.	**Paso 1** Observar si hay suficientes unidades para restar. Si no las hay, desagrupar una de las 6 decenas en 64 para obtener 10 unidades. 4 unidades más las 10 unidades nuevas son 14 unidades. Dibujamos una lupa alrededor del número superior para ayudar a los niños a concentrarse en desagrupar.

$$64 = 60 + 4$$
$$-28 = 20 + 8$$

Paso 2 Observar si hay suficientes unidades para restar. Si no las hay, desagrupar una decena para formar 10 unidades y sumarla a las unidades existentes.

$$64 = \overset{50}{\cancel{60}} + \overset{14}{\cancel{4}}$$
$$-28 = 20 + 8$$

Paso 2 Restar para hallar la respuesta. Los niños pueden restar de izquierda a derecha o de derecha a izquierda.

Paso 3 Restar para hallar la respuesta. Los niños pueden restar de izquierda a derecha o de derecha a izquierda.

$$64 = \overset{50}{\cancel{60}} + \overset{14}{\cancel{4}}$$
$$-28 = 20 + 8$$
$$\overline{30 + 6 = 36}$$

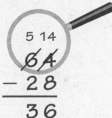

Cuando los niños expliquen el método que usan, deben hacerlo usando un lenguaje relacionado con "decenas y unidades". Esto demuestra que comprenden que están restando 2 decenas de 5 decenas (no 2 de 5) y 8 unidades de 14 unidades.

Si tiene alguna duda o algún comentario, por favor comuníquese conmigo.

Atentamente,

El maestro de su niño

 CA CC

En la Unidad 4 se aplican los siguientes estándares auxiliares, contenidos en los *Estándares estatales comunes de matemáticas con adiciones para California*: **2.OA.1, 2.OA.2, 2.NBT.4, 2.NBT.5, 2.NBT.6, 2.NBT.7, 2.NBT.7.1, 2.NBT.8, 2.NBT.9, 2.MD.8** y todos los de prácticas matemáticas.

4-5
Class Activity

Name

CA CC Content Standards 2.OA.1, 2.NBT.5, 2.NBT.7, 2.NBT.9
Mathematical Practices MP.1, MP.2, MP.4, MP.6

VOCABULARY
Expanded Method

▶ Explain the Expanded Method

Mr. Green likes this method. Explain what he does.

Step 1	Step 2	Step 3
$64 = 60 + 4$ $- 28 = 20 + 8$	$64 = \cancel{60}^{50} + \cancel{4}^{14}$ $- 28 = 20 + 8$	$64 = \cancel{60}^{50} + \cancel{4}^{14}$ $- 28 = 20 + 8$ $30 + 6 = 36$

▶ Try the Expanded Method

Show your work numerically and with a proof drawing.

1. $\begin{array}{r} 42 \\ -19 \\ \hline \end{array}$

2. $\begin{array}{r} 75 \\ -46 \\ \hline \end{array}$

3. $\begin{array}{r} 81 \\ -37 \\ \hline \end{array}$

VOCABULARY
Ungroup First Method

▶ Explain the Ungroup First Method

Mrs. Green likes this method. Explain what she does.

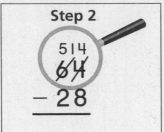

Step 1	Step 2	Step 3
64 − 28	5 1 4 6̸ 4̸ − 28	5 1 4 6̸ 4̸ − 28 —— 36

▶ Try the Ungroup First Method

Show your work numerically and with a proof drawing.

4.
```
 42
−19
```

5.
```
 75
−46
```

6.

```
 81
−37
```

Two Methods of Subtraction

▶ Solve and Discuss

Subtract to find the **difference.**

1.
$$
\begin{array}{r}
7\,5 \\
-\,4\,7 \\
\hline
\end{array}
$$

2.
$$
\begin{array}{r}
5\,4 \\
-\,1\,8 \\
\hline
\end{array}
$$

3.
$$
\begin{array}{r}
9\,4 \\
-\,3\,6 \\
\hline
\end{array}
$$

4.
$$
\begin{array}{r}
6\,6 \\
-\,3\,4 \\
\hline
\end{array}
$$

5.
$$
\begin{array}{r}
8\,5 \\
-\,5\,8 \\
\hline
\end{array}
$$

6.
$$
\begin{array}{r}
8\,9 \\
-\,6\,9 \\
\hline
\end{array}
$$

7.
$$
\begin{array}{r}
8\,2 \\
-\,5\,9 \\
\hline
\end{array}
$$

8.
$$
\begin{array}{r}
9\,7 \\
-\,7\,8 \\
\hline
\end{array}
$$

9.
$$
\begin{array}{r}
6\,5 \\
-\,2\,8 \\
\hline
\end{array}
$$

10.
$$
\begin{array}{r}
7\,8 \\
-\,1\,9 \\
\hline
\end{array}
$$

11.
$$
\begin{array}{r}
5\,3 \\
-\,2\,6 \\
\hline
\end{array}
$$

12.
$$
\begin{array}{r}
9\,1 \\
-\,4\,6 \\
\hline
\end{array}
$$

Name _____

▶ **What's the Error?**

$$
\begin{array}{r}
8\,\overset{13}{\cancel{3}} \\
-\,5\,5 \\
\hline
3\,8
\end{array}
$$

Did I make a mistake?

13. Show Puzzled Penguin how you would subtract. Draw a proof diagram to check your work.

$$
\begin{array}{r}
8\,3 \\
-\,5\,5 \\
\hline
\end{array}
$$

▶ **PATH to FLUENCY Add and Subtract Within 20**

Add.

14. $9 + 4 = \boxed{}$ **15.** $6 + 5 = \boxed{}$ **16.** $3 + 4 = \boxed{}$

17.
$$
\begin{array}{r}
8 \\
+\,7 \\
\hline
\end{array}
$$

18.
$$
\begin{array}{r}
4 \\
+\,8 \\
\hline
\end{array}
$$

19.
$$
\begin{array}{r}
5 \\
+\,9 \\
\hline
\end{array}
$$

Subtract.

20. $17 - 8 = \boxed{}$ **21.** $13 - 5 = \boxed{}$ **22.** $14 - 7 = \boxed{}$

23.
$$
\begin{array}{r}
9 \\
-\,6 \\
\hline
\end{array}
$$

24.
$$
\begin{array}{r}
1\,5 \\
-\,6 \\
\hline
\end{array}
$$

25.
$$
\begin{array}{r}
1\,6 \\
-\,8 \\
\hline
\end{array}
$$

Practice and Explain a Method

► Explain Ungrouping 200

Use this drawing to explain why 200 = 100 + 90 + 10.

► Review Both Methods

Expanded Method

$$
\begin{array}{r}
200 \\
- 68 \\
\end{array}
=
\begin{array}{c}
100 \quad 90 \quad 10 \\
200 + \cancel{0} + \cancel{0} \\
60 + 8 \\
\hline
\end{array}
\text{ or }
\begin{array}{c}
100 \quad 90 \quad 10 \\
200 + \cancel{0} + \cancel{0} \\
\end{array}
$$

$$100 + 30 + 2 = 132$$

Ungroup First Method

Ungroup in two steps.   or   Ungroup all at once.

Step 1. Ungroup 1 hundred to make 10 tens.

Step 2. Ungroup 1 ten to make 10 ones.

$$
\begin{array}{r}
\overset{9}{\cancel{1}}\overset{10\,10}{\cancel{200}} \\
- 68 \\
\hline
132 \\
\end{array}
\text{ or }
\begin{array}{r}
\overset{1\ 9\ 10}{\cancel{200}} \\
- 68 \\
\hline
132 \\
\end{array}
$$

Ungroup 1 hundred to make 9 tens and 10 ones.

$$200 = 100 + 90 + 10$$

Explain how ungrouping and subtraction work.

Relate the steps used in these methods to the drawing at the top of the page.

▶ Practice the Ungroup First Method

Use the Ungroup First Method to find each difference.

1.
```
  2 0 0
−   8 7
```

2.
```
  2 0 0
−   8 9
```

3.
```
  2 0 0
−   4 6
```

4.
```
  2 0 0
−   3 8
```

5.
```
  2 0 0
−   2 7
```

6.
```
  2 0 0
−   8 2
```

Subtract from 200

► **Decide When to Ungroup**

Decide if you need to ungroup. Then subtract.

1. 134
   − 78
   _____

   Did you ungroup a ten to
   get more ones? _____
   Did you ungroup a hundred
   to get more tens? _____

2. 134
   − 73
   _____

   Did you ungroup a ten to get
   more ones? _____
   Did you ungroup a hundred
   to get more tens? _____

3. 158
   − 37
   _____

   Did you ungroup a ten to get
   more ones? _____
   Did you ungroup a hundred
   to get more tens? _____

4. 138
   − 59
   _____

   Did you ungroup a ten to get
   more ones? _____
   Did you ungroup a hundred
   to get more tens? _____

5. 146
   − 57
   _____

   Did you ungroup a ten to get
   more ones? _____
   Did you ungroup a hundred
   to get more tens? _____

6. 146
   − 35
   _____

   Did you ungroup a ten to get
   more ones? _____
   Did you ungroup a hundred
   to get more tens? _____

▶ Decide When to Ungroup (continued)

Decide if you need to ungroup. Then subtract.

7. $\begin{array}{r} 1\,6\,7 \\ -\ \ 4\,2 \\ \hline \end{array}$

Did you ungroup a ten to get
more ones? _____
Did you ungroup a hundred
to get more tens? _____

8. $\begin{array}{r} 1\,4\,8 \\ -\ \ 3\,9 \\ \hline \end{array}$

Did you ungroup a ten to get
more ones? _____
Did you ungroup a hundred
to get more tens? _____

9. $\begin{array}{r} 1\,2\,4 \\ -\ \ 8\,6 \\ \hline \end{array}$

Did you ungroup a ten to get
more ones? _____
Did you ungroup a hundred
to get more tens? _____

10. $\begin{array}{r} 1\,5\,0 \\ -\ \ 2\,7 \\ \hline \end{array}$

Did you ungroup a ten to get
more ones? _____
Did you ungroup a hundred
to get more tens? _____

11. $\begin{array}{r} 1\,3\,9 \\ -\ \ 7\,5 \\ \hline \end{array}$

Did you ungroup a ten to get
more ones? _____
Did you ungroup a hundred
to get more tens? _____

12. $\begin{array}{r} 1\,7\,2 \\ -\ \ 6\,8 \\ \hline \end{array}$

Did you ungroup a ten to get
more ones? _____
Did you ungroup a hundred
to get more tens? _____

Ungroup from the Left or from the Right

▶ Subtract with Zeros

Decide if you need to ungroup. Then subtract.

1. $\begin{array}{r} 108 \\ -\ 46 \\ \hline \end{array}$

2. $\begin{array}{r} 103 \\ -\ 65 \\ \hline \end{array}$

3. $\begin{array}{r} 150 \\ -\ 79 \\ \hline \end{array}$

4. $\begin{array}{r} 102 \\ -\ 83 \\ \hline \end{array}$

5. $\begin{array}{r} 160 \\ -\ 92 \\ \hline \end{array}$

6. $\begin{array}{r} 107 \\ -\ 61 \\ \hline \end{array}$

7. $\begin{array}{r} 106 \\ -\ 38 \\ \hline \end{array}$

8. $\begin{array}{r} 170 \\ -\ 40 \\ \hline \end{array}$

9. $\begin{array}{r} 180 \\ -\ 93 \\ \hline \end{array}$

10. $\begin{array}{r} 140 \\ -\ 57 \\ \hline \end{array}$

11. $\begin{array}{r} 150 \\ -\ 84 \\ \hline \end{array}$

12. $\begin{array}{r} 106 \\ -\ 43 \\ \hline \end{array}$

▶ Solve and Discuss

Decide if you need to ungroup. Then subtract.

13.   1 0 6
     −   8 1
     ‾‾‾‾‾‾‾

14.   1 1 0
     −   1 8
     ‾‾‾‾‾‾‾

15.   1 9 0
     −   7 2
     ‾‾‾‾‾‾‾

16.   1 0 7
     −   3 8
     ‾‾‾‾‾‾‾

17.   1 3 0
     −   2 2
     ‾‾‾‾‾‾‾

18.   1 2 0
     −   6 3
     ‾‾‾‾‾‾‾

Solve each word problem. Make a
math drawing if you need more help.

Show your work.

19. Mr. Gordon sells cars. He wants to sell 109 cars
this month. So far he has sold 34 cars. How many
more cars does he need to sell?

☐ _____
       label

20. Mrs. Dash grilled 110 burgers for the
school picnic. 79 were eaten. How many
burgers are left?

☐ _____
       label

Name _____

CA CC Content Standards 2.NBT.1, 2.NBT.1a, 2.NBT.7, 2.NBT.9, 2.MD.8
Mathematical Practices MP.1, MP.2, MP.4, MP.6

► **Act it Out**

First, see how much money you have. Then decide what to buy. Pay for the item. Then write how much money you have left.

Yard Sale

| Cork Board 78¢ | Toy Rabbit 84¢ | Toy Guitar 75¢ | Perfume 89¢ | Knit Cap 99¢ |

1. I have 162¢ in my pocket.

   I bought the _____.

   $$\begin{array}{r} 1\ 6\ 2¢ \\ -\ \ \ \ \ \ ¢ \\ \hline \end{array}$$

   I have _____ ¢ left.

2. I have 143¢ in my pocket.

   I bought the _____.

   $$\begin{array}{r} 1\ 4\ 3¢ \\ -\ \ \ \ \ \ ¢ \\ \hline \end{array}$$

   I have _____ ¢ left.

3. I have 154¢ in my pocket.

   I bought the _____.

   $$\begin{array}{r} 1\ 5\ 4¢ \\ -\ \ \ \ \ \ ¢ \\ \hline \end{array}$$

   I have _____ ¢ left.

4. I have 126¢ in my pocket.

   I bought the _____.

   $$\begin{array}{r} 1\ 2\ 6¢ \\ -\ \ \ \ \ \ ¢ \\ \hline \end{array}$$

   I have _____ ¢ left.

▶ Use a Dollar Sign

Write the money amount. The first one is done for you.

5. 134¢ = _1_ dollar _3_ dimes _4_ pennies = $ _1_ . _3_ _4_

6. 76¢ = _____ dollars _____ dimes _____ pennies = $ _____ . _____ _____

7. 179¢ = _____ dollar _____ dimes _____ pennies = $ _____ . _____ _____

8. 58¢ = _____ dollars _____ dimes _____ pennies = $ _____ . _____ _____

Find the difference. Use play money to help you
ungroup, if you wish.

9.	10.	11.
$ 1 . 4 4 − . 2 3	$ 1 . 2 5 − . 9 5	$ 1 . 6 3 − . 9 5
12.	13.	14.
$ 1 . 5 8 − . 4 5	$ 1 . 3 6 − . 7 5	$ 1 . 9 2 − . 9 5

Model Subtraction with Money

Name _____

CA CC Content Standards 2.NBT.5
Mathematical Practices MP.1, MP.2, MP.5

► PATH to FLUENCY **Subtract Within 100**

Subtract.

1. $\begin{array}{r} 65 \\ -16 \\ \hline \end{array}$

2. $\begin{array}{r} 58 \\ -37 \\ \hline \end{array}$

3. $\begin{array}{r} 20 \\ -14 \\ \hline \end{array}$

4. $\begin{array}{r} 74 \\ -23 \\ \hline \end{array}$

5. $\begin{array}{r} 19 \\ -17 \\ \hline \end{array}$

6. $\begin{array}{r} 50 \\ -13 \\ \hline \end{array}$

7. $\begin{array}{r} 87 \\ -30 \\ \hline \end{array}$

8. $\begin{array}{r} 91 \\ -45 \\ \hline \end{array}$

9. $\begin{array}{r} 31 \\ -9 \\ \hline \end{array}$

10. $\begin{array}{r} 97 \\ -79 \\ \hline \end{array}$

11. $\begin{array}{r} 20 \\ -7 \\ \hline \end{array}$

12. $\begin{array}{r} 46 \\ -36 \\ \hline \end{array}$

Name _____

► PATH to FLUENCY **Subtract Within 100 (continued)**

Subtract.

13.
$$
\begin{array}{r}
1\,0\,0 \\
-\ \ 4\,8 \\
\hline
\end{array}
$$

14.
$$
\begin{array}{r}
6\,7 \\
-\,3\,1 \\
\hline
\end{array}
$$

15.
$$
\begin{array}{r}
5\,5 \\
-\,1\,6 \\
\hline
\end{array}
$$

16.
$$
\begin{array}{r}
8\,3 \\
-\ \ 8 \\
\hline
\end{array}
$$

17.
$$
\begin{array}{r}
4\,0 \\
-\,2\,6 \\
\hline
\end{array}
$$

18.
$$
\begin{array}{r}
1\,9 \\
-\,1\,1 \\
\hline
\end{array}
$$

19.
$$
\begin{array}{r}
1\,4 \\
-\,1\,1 \\
\hline
\end{array}
$$

20.
$$
\begin{array}{r}
2\,5 \\
-\,1\,2 \\
\hline
\end{array}
$$

21.
$$
\begin{array}{r}
1\,0\,0 \\
-\ \ 1\,9 \\
\hline
\end{array}
$$

22.
$$
\begin{array}{r}
9\,4 \\
-\,7\,6 \\
\hline
\end{array}
$$

23.
$$
\begin{array}{r}
2\,0 \\
-\ \ 8 \\
\hline
\end{array}
$$

24.
$$
\begin{array}{r}
7\,7 \\
-\,2\,4 \\
\hline
\end{array}
$$

Fluency: Subtraction Within 100

► PATH to FLUENCY **Ungroup Challenge**

Work in . Lay out Secret Code Cards like this.

10	60	1	6
1 0	6 0	1	6
2 0	7 0	2	7
3 0	8 0	3	8
4 0	9 0	4	9
5 0		5	

1. Use Secret Code Cards to help you make a 2-digit subtraction (top number less than 100).

2. Make another 2-digit subtraction.

• Use the same tens cards.

• If 👤 ungrouped a ten, use ones cards that *do not need more ones*.

• If 👤 did not ungroup a ten, use ones cards that *need more ones*.

Activity continues on next page.

© Houghton Mifflin Harcourt Publishing Company

► ^{PATH to FLUENCY} *Ungroup Challenge* (continued)

2. 👥 Work together to check your work.
Correct any errors.

3. Put the Secret Code Cards back. Switch
roles and repeat. Continue until time is up.

To play as a game and compete with another pair,
use the **Scoring Rules** *below.*

Scoring Rules

for

Ungroup Challenge

• Trade papers with another pair.

• Put a ✓ next to each correct answer.
Put an X next to each incorrect answer.

• Give I point for each ✓.
Subtract 3 points for each X.

• The pair with more points wins.

►Addition and Subtraction Word Problems

Draw a Math Mountain to solve each word problem. Show how you add or subtract.

Show your work.

1. Teresa has 45 blocks. Then she finds 29 more under the couch. How many blocks does Teresa have now?

☐ _____
   label

2. Krina's class makes 163 masks. They hang 96 of the masks in the library. How many masks do they have left?

☐ _____
   label

3. There are 12 girls and 8 boys in the library. How many children are in the library altogether?

☐ _____
   label

4. The school store has 90 glue sticks. Then 52 glue sticks are sold. How many glue sticks are left?

☐ _____
   label

▶ Addition and Subtraction Word Problems (continued)

Draw a Math Mountain to solve each word problem. Show how you add or subtract.

Show your work.

---

5. Sam has 47 marbles. Hank has 53 marbles. How many marbles do they have in all?

☐ _____
label

---

6. Mrs. Snap has 42 pencils. She gives 29 pencils to her students and puts the rest in a box. How many pencils does she put in the box?

☐ _____
label

---

7. At the park, Pam collects 25 leaves. Eighteen are oak leaves and the rest are maple leaves. How many are maple leaves?

☐ _____
label

---

8. Mr. Vazquez has 64 paintbrushes. He gives the art teacher 8 paintbrushes. How many paintbrushes does Mr. Vazquez have left?

☐ _____
label

CA CC Content Standards 2.OA.1, 2.NBT.5, 2.NBT.7
Mathematical Practices MP.1, MP.2, MP.4, MP.7, MP.8

▶ Find Equations for Math Mountains

1. Write all of the equations for 83, 59, and 24.

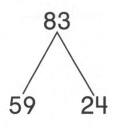

59 + 24 = 83

83 = 59 + 24

_____

_____

_____

_____

_____

_____

2. Write all of the equations for 142, 96, and 46.

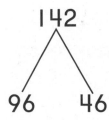

96 + 46 = 142

142 = 96 + 46

_____

_____

_____

_____

_____

_____

► Word Problem Practice: Addition and Subtraction Within 20

Make a drawing. Write an equation. Solve.

Show your work.

---

3. There are 7 children at the lunch table. Some more children sit down. Then there are 11 children at the table. How many children sit down?

☐ _____
　　　　　　label

---

4. Some leaves are on the ground. The children pick up 9 leaves. Then there are 3 leaves on the ground. How many leaves were on the ground at the start?

☐ _____
　　　　　　label

---

5. Teri has 5 more pencils than Adam. Adam has 6 pencils. How many pencils does Teri have?

☐ _____
　　　　　　label

---

6. Stevie has 8 more stickers than Ari. Stevie has 13 stickers. How many stickers does Ari have?

☐ _____
　　　　　　label

Equations with Greater Numbers

Name _____

CA CC Content Standards 2.OA.1, 2.NBT.1, 2.NBT.1a, 2.NBT.5, 2.NBT.6, 2.NBT.7.1, 2.NBT.9
Mathematical Practices MP.1, MP.2, MP.3, MP.6

► PATH to FLUENCY **Practice Addition and Subtraction Within 100**

Add or subtract. Watch the sign!

1.
$$\begin{array}{r} 91 \\ -63 \\ \hline \end{array}$$

2.
$$\begin{array}{r} 36 \\ +\ 9 \\ \hline \end{array}$$

3.
$$\begin{array}{r} 100 \\ -\ 74 \\ \hline \end{array}$$

4.
$$\begin{array}{r} 45 \\ +39 \\ \hline \end{array}$$

5.
$$\begin{array}{r} 64 \\ -23 \\ \hline \end{array}$$

6.
$$\begin{array}{r} 33 \\ +66 \\ \hline \end{array}$$

7.
$$\begin{array}{r} 20 \\ -\ 4 \\ \hline \end{array}$$

8.
$$\begin{array}{r} 34 \\ +38 \\ \hline \end{array}$$

9.
$$\begin{array}{r} 52 \\ -38 \\ \hline \end{array}$$

10.
$$\begin{array}{r} 43 \\ +57 \\ \hline \end{array}$$

11.
$$\begin{array}{r} 96 \\ -78 \\ \hline \end{array}$$

12.
$$\begin{array}{r} 13 \\ +79 \\ \hline \end{array}$$

►Solve and Discuss

Solve each word problem.

Show your work.

---

13. Tamyra bakes 48 muffins on Monday. On Tuesday she bakes 24 muffins. How many muffins does she bake during those two days?

☐ _____
     label

---

14. Mrs. Jennings gets 75 new books for the class library. She places 37 of them on the shelf. How many new books are left to place on the shelf?

☐ _____
     label

---

15. Isaac has 64 toy cars. Twenty-five of them are in a box. How many cars are not in the box?

☐ _____
     label

---

16. In June, Sarah reads 18 books. In July, she reads 35 books. How many books does she read in June and July?

☐ _____
     label

Practice Addition and Subtraction

VOCABULARY
estimate
round

► **Round** to the Nearest Ten

> Round 32 to the nearest ten. Follow these steps:
>
> **Step 1:** Underline the number in the tens' place. **32**
>
> **Step 2:** Write the ten that is greater than 32 above and write the ten that is less than 32 below.
>
> **Step 3:** Make a drawing to show each number.
>
> **Step 4:** If there are 5 or more ones, round up. If there are less than 5 ones, round down.

40 ||||

32 ||| ° °   2 is less than 5, so round down.

30 |||

► Practice Rounding

Round the number to the nearest ten.
You may use drawings.

17. 13 ☐

18. 18 ☐

19. 22 ☐

20. 44 ☐

21. 36 ☐

22. 55 ☐

▶ Round to Estimate Answers

Round each number to the nearest ten.
Then add or subtract the rounded numbers.
Circle the answer that is the better estimate.

23.
$$\begin{array}{r} 2\,1 \\ +\,1\,8 \\ \hline \end{array}$$

24.
$$\begin{array}{r} 4\,2 \\ +\,2\,3 \\ \hline \end{array}$$

25.
$$\begin{array}{r} 6\,7 \\ +\,1\,2 \\ \hline \end{array}$$

20 or 40   60 or 80   70 or 80

26.
$$\begin{array}{r} 4\,4 \\ -\,2\,2 \\ \hline \end{array}$$

27.
$$\begin{array}{r} 3\,8 \\ -\,1\,7 \\ \hline \end{array}$$

28.
$$\begin{array}{r} 5\,1 \\ -\,3\,8 \\ \hline \end{array}$$

10 or 20   20 or 30   10 or 30

Solve by rounding.   **Show your work.**

29. Jory has 3 large aquariums. These hold 28 fish,
    44 fish, and 13 fish. Round each number to the
    nearest 10. *About* how many fish does Jory have?

    about [ ] _____
                        label

30. At the picnic, 39 children chose apples and
    12 chose oranges. Round each number to
    the nearest 10. *About* how many more
    children chose apples than oranges?

    about [ ] _____
                        label

Practice Addition and Subtraction

▶ Introduce the Juice Bar

Grapefruit Juice 11¢	Red Apple Juice 41¢	Lemon Juice 20¢	Pear Juice 22¢
Green Apple Juice 25¢	Peach Juice 40¢	Orange Juice 18¢	Cantaloupe Juice 10¢
Pineapple Juice 47¢	Raspberry Juice 33¢	Banana Juice 39¢	Watermelon Juice 15¢
Grape Juice 50¢	Celery Juice 36¢	Tomato Juice 30¢	Carrot Juice 29¢

▶ Continue Buying and Selling

Choose two juice samples from the Juice Bar you would
like to mix together. Find the total cost. Then find the
change from one dollar.

1. I pick _____

   and _____.

   Juice 1 price: _____ ¢

   Juice 2 price: + _____ ¢

   Total: _____

   100¢ − _____ = _____

   My change is _____ ¢.

2. I pick _____

   and _____.

   Juice 1 price: _____ ¢

   Juice 2 price: + _____ ¢

   Total: _____

   100¢ − _____ = _____

   My change is _____ ¢.

3. I pick _____

   and _____.

   Juice 1 price: _____ ¢

   Juice 2 price: + _____ ¢

   Total: _____

   100¢ − _____ = _____

   My change is _____ ¢.

4. I pick _____

   and _____.

   Juice 1 price: _____ ¢

   Juice 2 price: + _____ ¢

   Total: _____

   100¢ − _____ = _____

   My change is _____ ¢.

Buy and Sell with One Dollar

▶ Practice the Adding Up Method

Add up to solve each word problem.

Show your work.

1. Doug has 62 baseball cards. After he goes shopping today, he will have 86 baseball cards. How many baseball cards is Doug going to buy?

   ☐ _____
      label

2. Myra has 87 dollars. She buys some gifts. Then she has 68 dollars. How much money does Myra spend on gifts?

   ☐ _____
      label

3. There are 15 apples in a basket. Some more apples are put in. Now there are 23 apples in the basket. How many apples are put in?

   ☐ _____
      label

4. Mr. Azim finds 113 golf balls. After he gives some to Carey, he has 54 golf balls left. How many golf balls does Mr. Azim give to Carey?

   ☐ _____
      label

▶ Practice the Adding Up Method (continued)

Add up to solve each word problem.

Show your work.

5. Frank has 27 sheets of green paper. He uses some to wrap presents. Then he has 18 sheets of green paper. How many sheets does he use?

[ ] _____
   label

6. There are 25 bikes at a store. Then some more bikes are brought to the store. Now there are 48 bikes at the store. How many bikes are brought to the store?

[ ] _____
   label

7. There are 95 pieces of popcorn in a bag. Jennifer eats some of the pieces. Now there are 52 pieces in the bag. How many pieces does Jennifer eat?

[ ] _____
   label

8. In a package of stickers, there are 45 red stickers and some blue stickers. There are 100 stickers in all. How many stickers are blue?

[ ] _____
   label

Name _____

CA CC Content Standards 2.OA.1, 2.NBT.5, 2.NBT.7, 2.NBT.9
Mathematical Practices MP.1, MP.6, MP.7

►Practice the Adding Up Method

Solve each word problem.

Show your work.

1. Justin reads 27 comics. Trina reads some comics. In all, they read 86 comics. How many comics does Trina read?

   [ ] _____
        label

2. Maya and Phillip draw 73 pictures. Maya draws 38 of the pictures. How many pictures does Phillip draw?

   [ ] _____
        label

3. There are 82 birds in the zoo. The zoo gets some more birds. Now they have 100 birds. How many birds does the zoo get?

   [ ] _____
        label

4. Mrs. Clark has 94 pens. She gives some pens to her friends. Now she has 75 pens. How many pens does Mrs. Clark give away?

   [ ] _____
        label

▶ Practice the Adding Up Method (continued)

Add up to solve each word problem.   **Show your work.**

5. Austin has 54 crayons. His sister gives him
some more crayons. Now he has 82 crayons.
How many crayons does his sister give him?

☐ _____
        label

6. In Robert's classroom, there are 39 books on a red shelf.
There are some books on a green shelf. There are 78 books
on the two shelves. How many books are on the green shelf?

☐ _____
        label

▶ (PATH to FLUENCY) Add and Subtract Within 100

Add.

7.	8.	9.	10.
22 + 30	17 + 3	51 + 34	86 + 9

Subtract.

11.	12.	13.	14.
100 − 68	92 − 15	83 − 77	54 − 29

More Word Problems with Unknown Addends

▶Solve Complex Word Problems

Write an equation. Solve the problem.

1. Marian has a collection of toy cars. She gives 28 cars to her brother Simon. Marian has 57 cars left. How many cars did she have to begin with?

　 _____
label

2. In September, Mr. Shaw planted some tulip bulbs. In October, he planted 35 more bulbs. Altogether he planted 81 bulbs. How many bulbs did he plant in September?

　 _____
label

3. Mrs. Lyle has a collection of 19 mugs. She buys some more. Now she has 34 mugs. How many mugs did Mrs. Lyle buy?

　 _____
label

4. Tarik picks 41 flowers. He gives some of the flowers to his aunt. He has 24 flowers left. How many flowers did Tarik give to his aunt ?

　 _____
label

▶ Solve Complex Word Problems (continued)

Write an equation. Solve the problem.

5. Frank has some markers.
   He buys 15 more markers.
   Now he has 62 markers. How
   many markers did Frank have
   to begin with?

   ┌──────┐
   │   │ _____
   └──────┘
        label

6. Kiki has 74 stickers. She gives
   some stickers to her friends.
   Now she has 29 stickers.
   How many stickers did Kiki give
   to her friends?

   ┌──────┐
   │   │ _____
   └──────┘
        label

7. Miss Harrod has a jar with some
   paperclips in it. She gives 53
   paperclips to the science teacher.
   There are 37 paperclips left in the
   jar. How many paperclips were
   in the jar before?

   ┌──────┐
   │   │ _____
   └──────┘
        label

8. Josef has 59 sports cards. His
   friend Tara gives him some more
   cards. Now Josef has 78 sports
   cards. How many cards did
   Tara give him?

   ┌──────┐
   │   │ _____
   └──────┘
        label

Start Unknown Problems

►Solve *Compare* Word Problems

Draw comparison bars and write an equation
to solve each problem.

1. Tia has 65 stamps. Stan has
29 stamps. How many more
stamps does Tia have than Stan?

2. Dora has 27 fewer grapes than
Jerry. Jerry has 72 grapes. How
many grapes does Dora have?

```
┌─────┐  _____
│     │
└─────┘       label
```

```
┌─────┐  _____
│     │
└─────┘       label
```

3. Lila has 34 snow globes in her
collection, which is 18 fewer
than her friend Betty has.
How many snow globes does
Betty have in her collection?

4. One year the Ricos planted 97
flowers. This was 29 more than
the Smiths planted. How many
flowers did the Smiths plant?

```
┌─────┐  _____
│     │
└─────┘       label
```

```
┌─────┐  _____
│     │
└─────┘       label
```

▶Solve *Compare* Word Problems (continued)

Draw comparison bars and write an equation
to solve each problem.

5. Pippa has 48 more beads than
Jeremy. Jeremy has 38 beads.
How many beads does
Pippa have?

6. In the classroom, there are
25 fiction books and 64 nonfiction
books. How many fewer fiction
books than nonfiction books are
in the classroom?

_____
label

_____
label

7. Boris has 16 more cherries than
Solongo. Boris has 60 cherries.
How many cherries does
Solongo have?

8. Mrs. Karimi has 36 fewer
crayons than Mr. Cabral.
Mrs. Karimi has 57 crayons.
How many crayons does
Mr. Cabral have?

_____
label

_____
label

▶ Solve and Discuss

Make a drawing. Write an equation. Solve.

1. Maxine cuts out 48 squares to make a quilt.
   She needs 16 more squares to complete the quilt.
   How many squares will be in the quilt altogether?

   ☐ _____
          label

2. Mr. Adams buys 93 paper plates for a party.
   He buys 43 large plates. The rest are small.
   How many small plates does he buy?

   ☐ _____
          label

3. Chad collects stamps. He has 32 stamps. Loren gives
   him some more stamps. Now Chad has 51 stamps.
   How many stamps did Loren give Chad?

   ☐ _____
          label

4. Trina's team scores 56 points at the basketball game.
   This is 30 more points than the other team scores.
   How many points does the other team score?

   ☐ _____
          label

► Solve and Discuss (continued)

Make a drawing. Write an equation. Solve.

---

5. Maura gives 19 trading cards to Jim. Now she
has 24 trading cards. How many trading cards
did Maura have to start?

☐ _____
       label

---

6. Jamal has 63 toy cars. Luis has 24 fewer toy cars
than Jamal. How many toy cars does Luis have?

☐ _____
       label

---

7. Anna has some red balloons and some blue balloons.
Altogether she has 46 balloons. How many balloons
of each color could she have?

☐ _____ and ☐ _____
       label   label

---

8. Jon has 71 stickers. Ken has 53 stickers. How
many fewer stickers does Ken have than Jon?

☐ _____
       label

Mixed Word Problems

▶ Solve and Discuss (continued)

Make a drawing. Write an equation. Solve.

---

9. Amanda has 22 more color pencils than Troy.
Troy has 38 color pencils. How many color
pencils does Amanda have?

☐ _____
        label

---

10. Nicole is matching spoons and forks. She finds
36 spoons and 50 forks. How many more spoons
does Nicole need to have the same number of
spoons as forks?

☐ _____
        label

---

11. Kristi has some shells. Then she finds 24 more
shells at the beach. Now Kristi has 100 shells.
How many shells did she start with?

☐ _____
        label

---

12. Gabby has 84 beads. She uses some beads to
make a necklace. Now she has 45 beads left.
How many beads does Gabby use to make
the necklace?

☐ _____
        label

► **What's the Error?**

Sona has 63 balloons. That is 16 more balloons than Molly. How many balloons does Molly have?

63 + 16 = 79
Sona   more   Molly

Did I make a mistake?

13. Draw comparison bars to help Puzzled Penguin. Write an equation to solve the problem.

Molly has ☐ balloons.

► PATH to FLUENCY **Add and Subtract Within 100**

Add.

14. 34
    + 46

15. 13
    + 78

16. 49
    + 26

Subtract.

17. 95
    − 38

18. 61
    − 28

19. 60
    − 33

Mixed Word Problems

Name _____

CA CC Content Standards 2.OA.1, 2.NBT.5
Mathematical Practices MP.1, MP.4, MP.6, MP.7

▶ Solve Two-Step Problems

Think about the first-step question.
Then solve the problem.

---

1. A farmer has two crates of milk bottles for sale.
   Each crate has 24 bottles. He sells 35 bottles.
   How many bottles of milk are left?

   ☐ _____
           label

---

2. There are 26 children at the library. 12 are girls and
   the rest are boys. Then 7 more boys come to the
   library. How many boys are at the library now?

   ☐ _____
           label

---

3. Jeff has 2 boxes of crayons and 15 other
   crayons. Each box contains 36 crayons.
   How many crayons does Jeff have altogether?

   ☐ _____
           label

► Solve Two-Step Problems (continued)

Think about the first-step question.
Then solve the problem.

---

4. Whitney collects 18 cans for recycling. Tara collects 9 cans. Julia collects 12 more cans than Whitney and Tara collect together. How many cans does Julia collect?

☐ _____
      label

---

5. Margie has 17 balloons. Logan has 9 more balloons than Margie. Bonnie has 12 fewer balloons than Logan. How many balloons does Bonnie have?

☐ _____
      label

---

6. Mr. Tyson makes 75 rings to sell at a fair. He sells 16 rings on the first day. He sells some more on the second day. Now he has 22 rings left. How many rings did Mr. Tyson sell on the second day?

☐ _____
      label

Name _____

CA CC Content Standards 2.OA.1, 2.NBT.5
Mathematical Practices MP.1, MP.2, MP.3, MP.6

▶ Solve Two-Step Problems

Think about the first-step question.
Then solve the problem.

1. Lin gets $38 for babysitting. She spends $12 on a present for her mother and puts the rest in a money jar. She then gives some money to her sister. Now she has $18. How many dollars did Lin give her sister?

$$\boxed{}\ \underline{\hspace{4cm}}$$
label

2. Russell has 28 marbles. Ridge has 12 fewer marbles than Russell. Natasha has as many marbles as Russell and Ridge together. How many marbles does Natasha have?

$$\boxed{}\ \underline{\hspace{4cm}}$$
label

3. Mr. Verdi is sewing costumes for the school play. He needs 26 blue buttons. He also needs 16 green buttons and 34 red buttons. How many buttons does Mr. Verdi need in all?

$$\boxed{}\ \underline{\hspace{4cm}}$$
label

▶ Solve Two-Step Problems (continued)

Think about the first-step question.
Then solve the problem.

4. Jolinda starts with 56 patches for her quilt. 25 are red
   and the rest are green. She adds some more green
   patches to the quilt. Now there are 36 green patches
   in her quilt. How many green patches does Jolinda
   add to the quilt?

   _____
   label

5. Gabe and Juan find 32 feathers. Mari and Kaila find
   12 more feathers than Gabe and Juan. If Mari finds
   19 feathers, how many feathers does Kaila find?

   _____
   label

6. Kyle plants 15 seeds in the first pot. He plants
   12 seeds in the second pot and 18 seeds in the third
   pot. The fourth pot is large. He plants as many seeds
   in the fourth pot as in all the other three pots. How
   many seeds does Kyle plant in the four pots altogether?

   _____
   label

More Two-Step Problems

4-23
Class Activity

Name _____

CA CC Content Standards 2.OA.1, 2.NBT.5, 2.NBT.7, 2.MD.1, 2.MD.3, 2.MD.4, 2.MD.5 Mathematical Practices MP.1, MP.2, MP.3, MP.4, MP.5, MP.6

▶ Math and Dinosaurs

The Stegosaurus was a large plant-eating dinosaur. It had two rows of plates running along its back and long spikes on its tail.

The feet of the Stegosaurus were short and wide. The forefeet (the feet on the front legs) had five short, wide toes with short hoof-like tips. The rear feet had three short, wide toes with hooves.

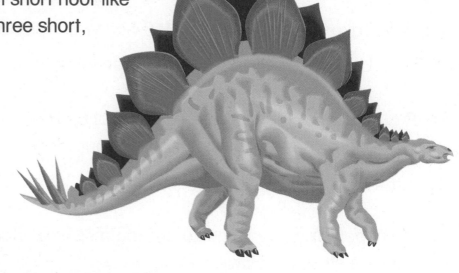

1. The rear foot of a Stegosaurus was about 35 centimeters long. Use scissors and tape to make a paper strip that is 35 centimeters long. Write on the strip: *Foot of Stegosaurus.*

2. Now measure your own foot in centimeters.

    My foot is ☐ centimeters long.

    Make a paper strip that is the same length as your foot. Write on the strip: *My Foot.*

3. How much longer is the foot of the Stegosaurus than your foot?

    ☐ centimeters

▶ Measure Stride

4. Work with a partner to measure your *stride*.

STEP 1. Put a piece of tape on the floor.

STEP 2. Line up your right and left heels with the edge of the tape.

STEP 3. Take a normal walking step with your left foot.

STEP 4. Take a normal walking step with your right foot.

STEP 5. Use tape to mark where the heel of your right foot lands.

STEP 6. Measure the distance in centimeters between the two pieces of tape. This is your *stride*.

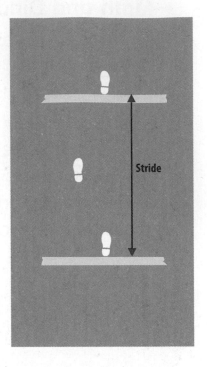

My stride is ☐ centimeters long.

Make a paper strip that is the same length as your stride. Write on the strip: *My Stride.*

5. The stride of the Stegosaurus is measured using footprints from its right hind leg. Its stride was about 190 centimeters. Make a paper strip that is 190 centimeters long. Write on it: *Stride of Stegosaurus.*

6. How much longer is the stride of the Stegosaurus than your stride?

☐ centimeters

7. Compare your stride with your partner's stride.

Who has the longer stride? _____

How much longer is it? ☐ centimeters

Subtract. Match each subtraction to its answer.

1.
$$\begin{array}{r} 74 \\ -\ 38 \\ \hline \end{array}$$ •
• 46

$$\begin{array}{r} 63 \\ -\ 17 \\ \hline \end{array}$$ •
• 39

$91 - 52$ •
• 36

Is the answer correct? Choose Yes or No.

2.
$$\begin{array}{r} 1\ 7 \\ -\ 4 \\ \hline 1\ 2 \end{array}$$ ○ Yes   ○ No

$$\begin{array}{r} 2\ 0 \\ -\ 9 \\ \hline 1\ 1 \end{array}$$ ○ Yes   ○ No

$$\begin{array}{r} 4\ 1 \\ -\ 7 \\ \hline 3\ 4 \end{array}$$ ○ Yes   ○ No

3. Hector has 1 dollar, 2 quarters, 1 dime, 3 nickels, and 1 penny.

Draw 100 s, 25 s, 10 s, 5 s, 1 s

Write the total amount of money. $ _____ . _____ _____

total

Name _____

Under each picture, write the total amount of money so far. Then write the total using $.

4.

| 25¢ | 25¢ | 25¢ | 10¢ | 10¢ | 10¢ |

_25¢_   _50¢_   _____   _____   _____   _____

$ _____ . _____ _____

total

Round the number to the nearest ten.
You may use drawings.

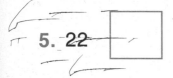

5. 22 [ ]   6. 84 [ ]

7. 57 [ ]   8. 68 [ ]

Round each number to the nearest ten.
Then add or subtract the rounded numbers.
Circle the answer that is the better estimate.

| 9. 32
 + 16 | 10. 63
 + 11 | 11. 58
 − 33 | 12. 79
 − 26 |

30 or 50   70 or 80   20 or 30   50 or 60

Do you need to ungroup to subtract?
Choose Yes or No.

13. $\begin{array}{r} 140 \\ -\ 89 \\ \hline \end{array}$

○ Yes   ○ No

$\begin{array}{r} 200 \\ -\ 54 \\ \hline \end{array}$

○ Yes   ○ No

Solve.

Show your work.

14. Jaime, David, and Taylor have beads to make key chains. Jaime has 24 beads. David has 12 more beads than Jaime. Taylor has 14 fewer beads than David. How many beads does Taylor have?

☐ _____
   label

15. Charlotte, Dustin, and Randy are picking peaches. Charlotte picks 14 peaches, Dustin picks 28 peaches, and Randy picks 23 peaches. How many peaches do they pick?

☐ _____
   label

16. There are 27 marbles in a bag. Kim puts more marbles into the bag. Now there are 59 marbles in the bag. How many marbles does Kim put into the bag?

☐ _____
   label

17. Brad subtracts 65 from 151. Should he follow the steps listed below? Choose Yes or No.

Ungroup 5 tens as 4 tens 10 ones.	○ Yes	○ No
Subtract 5 ones from 10 ones.	○ Yes	○ No
Subtract 6 tens from 4 tens.	○ Yes	○ No
Subtract 6 tens from 14 tens.	○ Yes	○ No

18. Jeff wants to buy a baseball card for $1.52. Show two ways he could pay for the baseball card.

☐ dollars ☐ quarters ☐ dimes

☐ nickels ☐ pennies

☐ dollars ☐ quarters ☐ dimes

☐ nickels ☐ pennies

19. Subtract 38 from 57. Explain all the steps you use.

$$\begin{array}{r} 57 \\ -\ 38 \\ \hline \end{array}$$

Family Letter

Content Overview

Dear Family:

Your child is beginning a new unit on time.

You can help your child link the time concepts learned in school with the real world.

Together, look for clocks in your home. You might search for watches, alarm clocks, digital clocks, and clocks on appliances.

Talk about time throughout your family's day. For example, you can point to the clock during breakfast and say, "We usually eat breakfast at this time. It is 7:30 A.M."

In this unit, your child will learn to tell time to the hour, half hour, and five minutes. Your child will practice writing the time.

If you have any questions or comments, please call or write to me. Thank you.

Sincerely,
Your child's teacher

CA CC

Unit 5 addresses the following standards from the *Common Core State Standards for Mathematics with California Additions*: **2.OA.1, 2.OA.2, 2.NBT.2, 2.NBT.4, 2.NBT.5, 2.MD.7, 2.MD.10, 2.G.3,** and all Mathematical Practices.

Estimada familia:

Su niño está empezando una unidad donde aprenderá sobre la hora.

Usted puede ayudarlo a que conecte los conceptos relacionados con la hora que aprendió en la escuela, con el mundo real.

Busquen juntos relojes en la casa. Puede buscar relojes de pulsera, relojes con alarma, relojes digitales y relojes que estén en los electrodomésticos.

Durante un día en familia, hablen de la hora. Por ejemplo, puede señalar un reloj durante el desayuno y decir: "Generalmente desayunamos a esta hora. Son las 7:30 a.m."

En esta unidad su niño aprenderá a leer la hora en punto, la media hora y los cinco minutos para la hora. Su niño practicará cómo escribir la hora.

Si tiene alguna pregunta o algún comentario, por favor comuníquese conmigo. Gracias.

Atentamente,
El maestro de su niño

CA CC

En la Unidad 5 se aplican los siguientes estándares auxiliares, contenidos en los *Estándares estatales comunes de matemáticas con adiciones para California*: **2.OA.1, 2.OA.2, 2.NBT.2, 2.NBT.4, 2.NBT.5, 2.MD.7, 2.MD.10, 2.G.3** y todos los de prácticas matemáticas.

Name _____

CA CC Content Standards 2.MD.7
Mathematical Practices MP.2, MP.5, MP.6

► **Features of Clocks**

Clocks are tools that we use to measure time.

1. Describe some clocks that you have seen.

_____

_____

_____

Place the missing numbers on the **analog clocks**.

2.

3.

4.

An analog clock has a long hand that is the **minute hand**
and a short hand that is the **hour hand**.
Ring the hour hand on the clocks.

5.

6.

7.

Ring the minute hand on the clocks.

8.

9.

10.

VOCABULARY
A.M.
P.M.

►Times of Daily Activities

We use **A.M.** for the hours after 12:00 midnight and before 12:00 noon.
9:00 A.M. is 9 o'clock in the morning.

We use **P.M.** for the hours after 12:00 noon and before 12:00 midnight.
9:00 P.M. is 9 o'clock in the evening.

11. Complete the chart. For each time listed, write whether it is dark or light outside; whether it is morning, afternoon, or evening; and an activity you might be doing at that time.

Time	Sunlight	Part of the Day	Activity
4:00 A.M.	dark	morning	sleeping
12:30 P.M.			
9:00 P.M.			

For each activity, ring the most appropriate time.

12. brush your teeth in the morning

   1:30 P.M.   3:00 P.M.   7:30 A.M.

13. eat dinner at night

   5:00 A.M.   12:00 noon   6:00 P.M.

14. watch an afternoon movie

   3:00 A.M.   2:00 P.M.   6:00 P.M.

► Model a Clock

Attach the clock hands using a prong fastener.

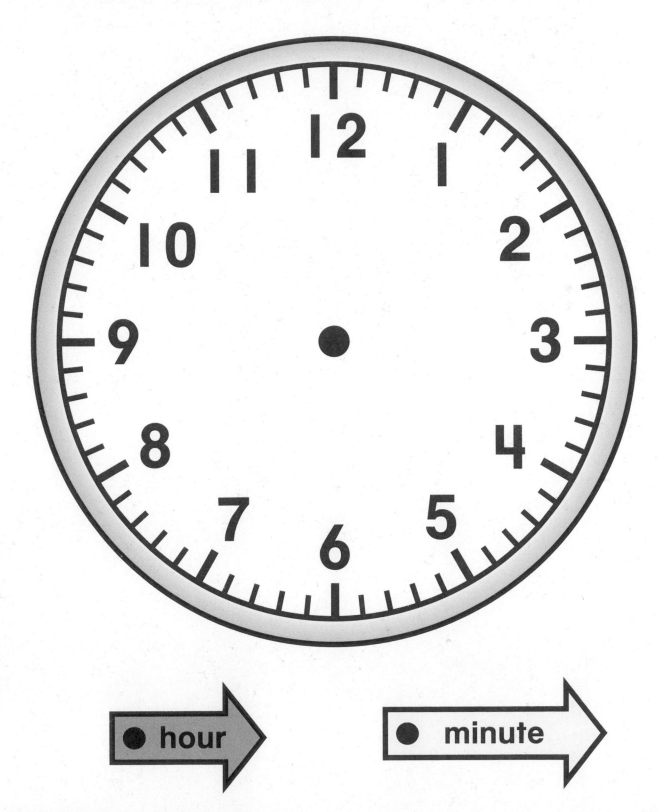

VOCABULARY
digital clock

►Write Time

On a **digital clock**, the number on the left shows the hour, and the number on the right shows the minutes after the hour.

hour   minutes

Write the time in two different ways.

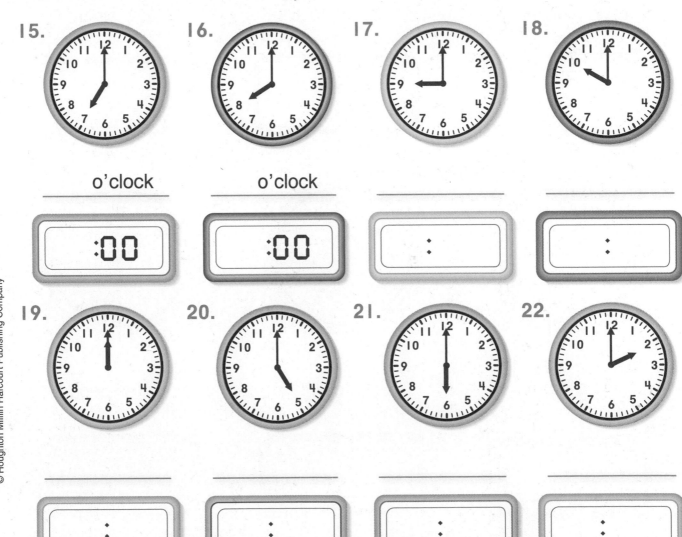

15.

16.

17.

18.

o'clock

o'clock

:00

:00

:

:

19.

20.

21.

22.

:

:

:

:

▶ Draw Clock Hands

Draw the hands on each analog clock, and write
the time on each digital clock below.

23.

7 o'clock

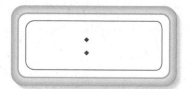

24.

11 o'clock

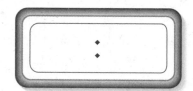

25.

2 o'clock

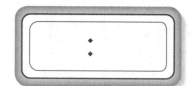

26.

3 o'clock

27.

5 o'clock

28.

10 o'clock

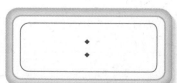

Hours and A.M. or P.M.

▶ 5-Minute Intervals

I. Count by 5s around the clock.

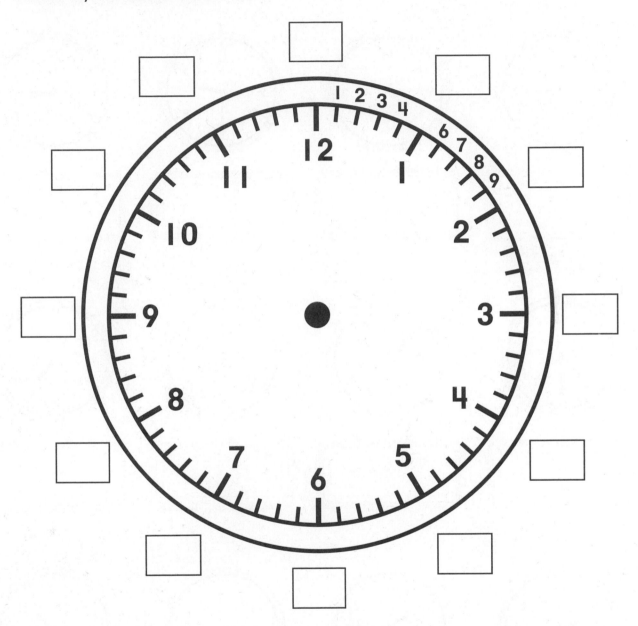

► Read Time to 5 Minutes

Write the time on the digital clocks.

2.

3.

4.

5.

6.

7.

8.

9.

10.

11.
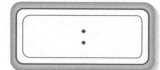

12.

13.

► Show Times to 5 Minutes

Draw hands on each clock to show the time.

14.

`10:35`

15.

`9:20`

16.

`2:25`

17.

`4:50`

18.

`7:05`

19.

`3:30`

20.

`5:50`

21.

`8:00`

22.

`10:15`

23.

`12:25`

24.

`3:55`

25.

`4:30`

► What's the Error?

Did I make a mistake?

26. What is the correct time?

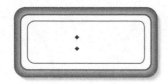

► A.M. or P.M.?

For each activity, ring the appropriate time.

27. picnic	**28.** school recess	**29.** afternoon snack	**30.** going to the playground
5:30 A.M.	10:00 A.M.	3:15 A.M.	9:25 A.M.
5:30 P.M.	10:00 P.M.	3:15 P.M.	9:25 P.M.

31. lunch	**32.** sunset	**33.** wake up	**34.** math class
12:10 A.M.	7:05 A.M.	6:45 A.M.	8:30 A.M.
12:10 P.M.	7:05 P.M.	6:45 P.M.	8:30 P.M.

► Understand Relationships of Time and the Calendar

Write the correct number.

35. I hour = ☐ minutes   **36.** I day = ☐ hours

37. I week = ☐ days

Complete the names of the days of the week.

38. Sunday

M_____

T_____

W_____

T_____

F_____

S_____

Complete the following.

39. March has ☐ days.

Circle March 6 and March 16.

Put an X over every Saturday.

What day of the week is March 12?

_____

What day of the week is March 29?

_____

March						
S	M	T	W	T	F	S
				1	2	3
4	5	6	7	8	9	10
11	12	13	14	15	16	17
18	19	20	21	22	23	24
25	26	27	28	29	30	31

January
S	M	T	W	T	F	S
	1	2	3	4	5	6
7	8	9	10	11	12	13
14	15	16	17	18	19	20
21	22	23	24	25	26	27
28	29	30	31			

February
S	M	T	W	T	F	S
				1	2	3
4	5	6	7	8	9	10
11	12	13	14	15	16	17
18	19	20	21	22	23	24
25	26	27	28			

March
S	M	T	W	T	F	S
				1	2	3
4	5	6	7	8	9	10
11	12	13	14	15	16	17
18	19	20	21	22	23	24
25	26	27	28	29	30	31

April
S	M	T	W	T	F	S
1	2	3	4	5	6	7
8	9	10	11	12	13	14
15	16	17	18	19	20	21
22	23	24	25	26	27	28
29	30					

May
S	M	T	W	T	F	S
	1	2	3	4	5	
6	7	8	9	10	11	12
13	14	15	16	17	18	19
20	21	22	23	24	25	26
27	28	29	30	31		

June
S	M	T	W	T	F	S
					1	2
3	4	5	6	7	8	9
10	11	12	13	14	15	16
17	18	19	20	21	22	23
24	25	26	27	28	29	30

July
S	M	T	W	T	F	S
1	2	3	4	5	6	7
8	9	10	11	12	13	14
15	16	17	18	19	20	21
22	23	24	25	26	27	28
29	30	31				

August
S	M	T	W	T	F	S
			1	2	3	4
5	6	7	8	9	10	11
12	13	14	15	16	17	18
19	20	21	22	23	24	25
26	27	28	29	30	31	

September
S	M	T	W	T	F	S
						1
2	3	4	5	6	7	8
9	10	11	12	13	14	15
16	17	18	19	20	21	22
23	24	25	26	27	28	29
30						

October
S	M	T	W	T	F	S
	1	2	3	4	5	6
7	8	9	10	11	12	13
14	15	16	17	18	19	20
21	22	23	24	25	26	27
28	29	30	31			

November
S	M	T	W	T	F	S
				1	2	3
4	5	6	7	8	9	10
11	12	13	14	15	16	17
18	19	20	21	22	23	24
25	26	27	28	29	30	

December
S	M	T	W	T	F	S
						1
2	3	4	5	6	7	8
9	10	11	12	13	14	15
16	17	18	19	20	21	22
23	24	25	26	27	28	29
30	31					

40. How many months are in one year? [   ] months

41. Which months have 31 days? _____

_____

Which months have only 30 days? _____

_____

Which month has fewer than 30 days? _____

Family Letter

Content Overview

Dear Family:

Your child is learning how to show information in various ways. In this unit, children will learn how to create and read picture graphs and bar graphs.

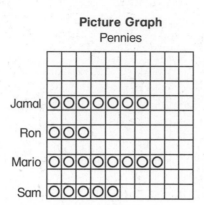

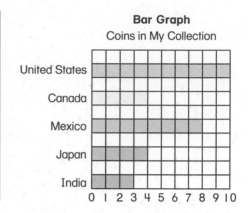

An important feature of *Math Expressions* is its emphasis on real world connections. Children will collect and represent data on graphs. They will also interpret the graph to answer questions about the data shown.

Children also explore the language of comparison by using such words as *same, more, less,* and *fewer*. The connection between pairs of terms is emphasized. For example: Carlos has 8 stickers. Maria has 3. Carlos has 5 *more* stickers than Maria. Maria has 5 *fewer* stickers than Carlos has.

Please call if you have any questions or concerns. Thank you for helping your child learn how to create, read, and interpret graphs.

Sincerely,
Your child's teacher

© Houghton Mifflin Harcourt Publishing Company

CA CC

Unit 5 addresses the following standards from the *Common Core State Standards for Mathematics with California Additions*: **2.OA.1, 2.OA.2, 2.NBT.2, 2.NBT.4, 2.NBT.5, 2.MD.7, 2.MD.10, 2.G.3,** and all Mathematical Practices.

Estimada familia:

Su niño está aprendiendo a mostrar información de varias maneras. En esta unidad los niños aprenderán a crear y a leer gráficas de dibujos y gráficas de barras.

Gráfica de dibujos
Monedas de 1 centavo

Jamal ○○○○○○
Ron ○○○
Mario ○○○○○○○
Sam ○○○○

Gráfica de barras
Monedas de mi colección

Estados Unidos
Canadá
México
Japón
India
0 1 2 3 4 5 6 7 8 9 10

Un aspecto importante de *Math Expressions* es su énfasis en las conexiones con situaciones de la vida cotidiana. Los niños reunirán datos y los representarán en gráficas. También interpretarán las gráficas para responder preguntas acerca de los datos que se muestran.

Los niños también estudiarán palabras que se usan para comparar, tales como *igual, mismo, más* y *menos*. Se hará énfasis en la conexión entre los pares de términos. Por ejemplo: Carlos tiene 8 adhesivos. María tiene 3. Carlos tiene 5 adhesivos *más* que María. María tiene 5 adhesivos *menos* que Carlos.

Si tiene alguna pregunta o algún comentario, por favor comuníquese conmigo. Gracias por ayudar a su niño a aprender cómo crear, leer e interpretar gráficas.

Atentamente,
El maestro de su niño

CA CC

En la Unidad 5 se aplican los siguientes estándares auxiliares, contenidos en los *Estándares estatales comunes de matemáticas con adiciones para California*: **2.OA.1, 2.OA.2, 2.NBT.2, 2.NBT.4, 2.NBT.5, 2.MD.7, 2.MD.10, 2.G.3** y todos los de prácticas matemáticas.

CA CC Content Standards 2.0A.1, 2.MD.10
Mathematical Practices MP.1

VOCABULARY
picture graph

▶ Use Picture Graphs to Compare Amounts

Read the **picture graph**.

Write the number. Ring *more* or *fewer*.

Number of Balloons	
Carla	🎈🎈🎈🎈🎈🎈🎈
Peter	🎈🎈🎈🎈
Hanna	🎈🎈🎈🎈🎈

1. Carla has ☐ *more fewer* balloons than Peter.

2. Hanna has ☐ *more fewer* balloons than Carla.

Read the picture graph. Write the number.

Leaves Collected	
Amari	🍂🍂🍂🍂
Sam	🍂🍂🍂🍂🍂🍂🍂🍂
Marco	🍂🍂🍂🍂🍂🍂

3. Amari needs ☐ more leaves to have as many as Sam has.

4. If Sam gives away ☐ leaves, he will have as many leaves as Marco has.

► Solve *Put Together/Take Apart* **Problems**

This picture graph shows the number of apples
Mrs. Reid bought at the store.

5. How many apples did Mrs. Reid
buy altogether?

☐ . _____
    label

Apples Bought				
Red	🍎	🍎	🍎	🍎
Green	🍎	🍎		
Yellow	🍏	🍏		

6. There are 2 green apples, I yellow apple, and I red
apple in the bowl. The rest are in Mrs. Reid's bag.
How many apples are in the bag?

☐ _____
   label

This picture graph shows the number of
books that four children read.

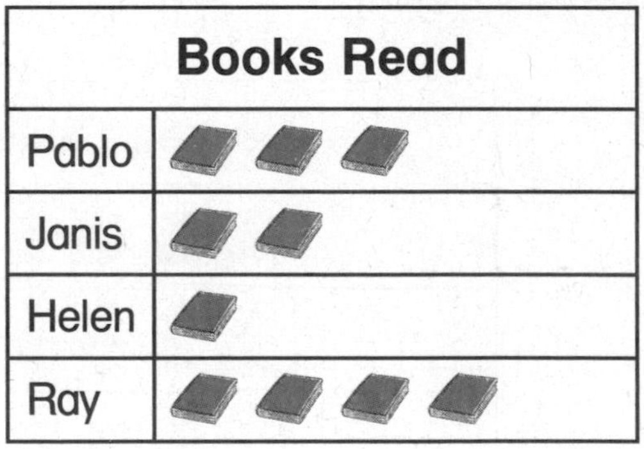

7. Two children read 6 books altogether.
Who are the two children?

_____ and _____

Books Read				
Pablo	📕	📕	📕	
Janis	📕	📕		
Helen	📕			
Ray	📕	📕	📕	📕

8. Two of the books the children read are about cars and
2 books are about trains. The rest of the books are about
animals. How many books are about animals?

☐ _____
   label

Read Picture Graphs

5-5
Class Activity

Name _____

CA CC Content Standards 2.OA.1, 2.NBT.5, 2.MD.10
Mathematical Practices MP.1, MP.2, MP.4, MP.6

VOCABULARY
bar graph

▶ Make a Picture Graph

Title: _____

▶ Make a Bar Graph

Title: _____

▶ **PATH to FLUENCY** **Add and Subtract Within 100**

Add.

1. $46 + 4 = $ _____   2. $3 + 39 = $ _____   3. $26 + 71 = $ _____

$$
\begin{array}{r} 4. \quad 56 \\ + 36 \\ \hline \end{array}
\qquad
\begin{array}{r} 5. \quad 11 \\ + 47 \\ \hline \end{array}
\qquad
\begin{array}{r} 6. \quad 36 \\ + 53 \\ \hline \end{array}
\qquad
\begin{array}{r} 7. \quad 78 \\ + \ 6 \\ \hline \end{array}
$$

$$
\begin{array}{r} 8. \quad 25 \\ + 61 \\ \hline \end{array}
\qquad
\begin{array}{r} 9. \quad 18 \\ + 60 \\ \hline \end{array}
\qquad
\begin{array}{r} 10. \quad 44 \\ + 17 \\ \hline \end{array}
\qquad
\begin{array}{r} 11. \quad 13 \\ + \ 5 \\ \hline \end{array}
$$

Subtract.

12. $74 - 8 = $ _____   13. $51 - 12 = $ _____   14. $60 - 15 = $ _____

$$
\begin{array}{r} 15. \quad 42 \\ - 34 \\ \hline \end{array}
\qquad
\begin{array}{r} 16. \quad 78 \\ - 29 \\ \hline \end{array}
\qquad
\begin{array}{r} 17. \quad 43 \\ - 28 \\ \hline \end{array}
\qquad
\begin{array}{r} 18. \quad 50 \\ - 18 \\ \hline \end{array}
$$

$$
\begin{array}{r} 19. \quad 80 \\ - 37 \\ \hline \end{array}
\qquad
\begin{array}{r} 20. \quad 64 \\ - 45 \\ \hline \end{array}
\qquad
\begin{array}{r} 21. \quad 28 \\ - 14 \\ \hline \end{array}
\qquad
\begin{array}{r} 22. \quad 56 \\ - 27 \\ \hline \end{array}
$$

     Introduce Bar Graphs

Name _____

CA CC Content Standards 2.0A.1, 2.MD.10
Mathematical Practices MP.1, MP.3, MP.6, MP.7

► Read a **Horizontal Bar Graph**

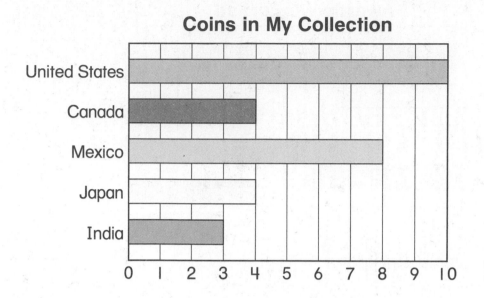

Coins in My Collection

► Read a **Vertical Bar Graph**

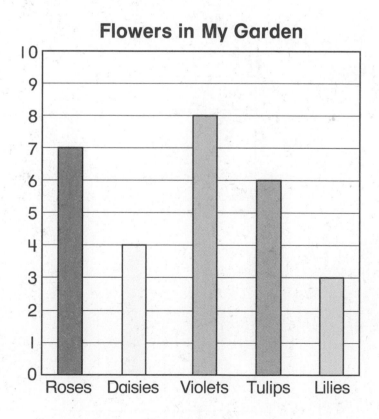

Flowers in My Garden

► Write Comparison Statements

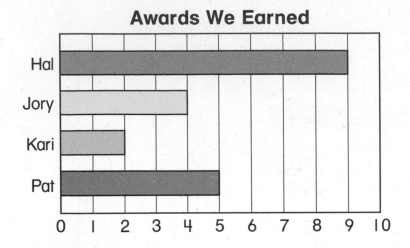

Awards We Earned

1. Use the horizontal bar graph.
   Write an *is greater than* statement.

_____

_____

► Make a Vertical Bar Graph

2. Make a vertical bar graph
   from the horizontal
   bar graph above.

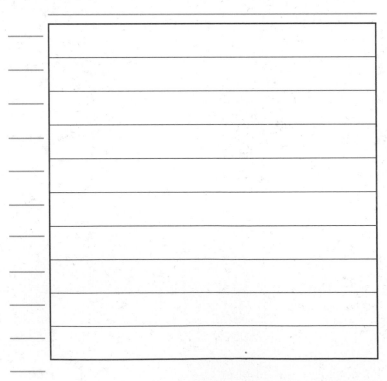

► Solve *Put Together/Take Apart* and *Compare* Problems

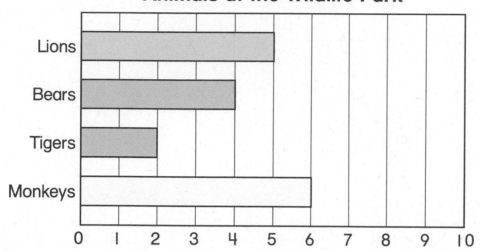

Animals at the Wildlife Park

Use the bar graph to solve the problems.

Show your work.

1. Four of the monkeys are adults and the rest are babies. How many of the monkeys are babies?

☐ _____
    label

2. How many fewer bears are there than monkeys?

☐ _____
    label

3. There are 2 fewer lions than elephants. How many elephants are there?

☐ _____
    label

▶ Solve Word Problems with More Than One Step

Jenny's Bead Collection

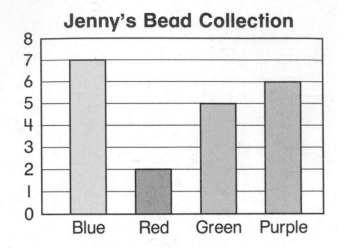

Use the bar graph to solve the problems.

Show your work.

4. Jenny has 4 fewer purple beads than Morgan.
   How many purple beads do Jenny and Morgan
   have in all?

   ☐ _____
   label

5. Morgan has 11 red beads. Then she gives 2 red
   beads to Arun. How many more red beads does
   Morgan have now than Jenny?

   ☐ _____
   label

6. Five of Jenny's beads are large and the rest
   are small. She buys some small yellow beads.
   Now she has 18 small beads. How many small
   yellow beads does she buy?

   ☐ _____
   label

© Houghton Mifflin Harcourt Publishing Company

► **What's the Error?**

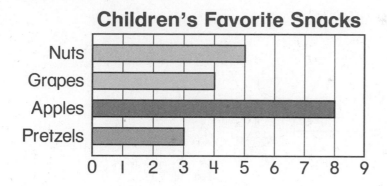

Children's Favorite Snacks

How many more children
choose fruit than nuts?

Fruit | 8
Nuts | 5 | ?

$8 - 5 = 3$

3 more children

Am I correct?

7. Show Puzzled Penguin how you
   would solve the problem.

[ ] more children

► Organize and Graph Information

Here are some shapes for you to graph.

8. First make a **table**.

9. Then make a bar graph.

	Number

Solve Problems Using a Bar Graph

VOCABULARY
survey
data

▶ Record the Collected Data

1. Show the results of your **survey** in the table. Your teacher will help you.

_____	Number of Children

2. Show the **data** on a picture graph.

_____

3. Show the data on a bar graph.

_____

4. Use the data to write a 2-step word problem.

_____

_____

► What's the Error?

Favorite Subject	Number of Children
Reading	6
Math	7
Science	4
Art	4

Puzzled Penguin made a graph from the table.

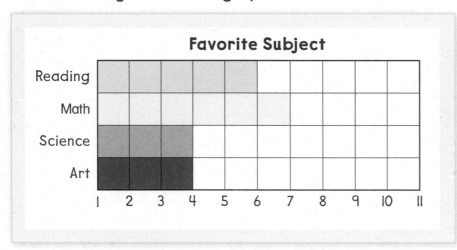

5. Fix Puzzled Penguin's errors.

► PATH to FLUENCY Add and Subtract Within 100

Add.

6. 76
 + 17

7. 49
 + 21

8. 12
 + 51

Subtract.

9. 86
 − 28

10. 60
 − 37

11. 46
 − 19

Name _____

CA CC Content Standards 2.OA.1, 2.MD.10
Mathematical Practices MP.1, MP.3, MP.4, MP.6

►Make Graphs Using Data from a Table

The table shows the number of bicycles sold at a store
on four days last week.

Bicycle Sales

Day	Number Sold
Saturday	8
Sunday	9
Monday	3
Tuesday	4

1. Make a picture graph using data from the table.

2. Make a bar graph using data from the table.

► Solve Problems Using a Bar Graph

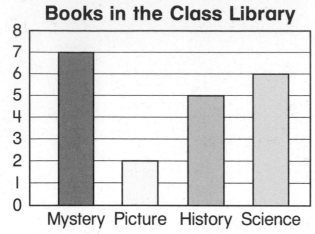

Books in the Class Library

Use the bar graph to solve the problems.

Show your work.

3. Children are reading 3 history books.
   The rest are on the shelf in the library.
   How many history books are on the shelf?

   ☐ _____
         label

4. The class library has 2 more science books than
   math books. How many more math books must
   the library get so there is the same number of
   math books as mystery books?

   ☐ _____
         label

5. Children are reading some of the mystery books.
   The rest are on the shelf. The library gets 6 new
   mystery books. Now there are 10 mystery books on the
   shelf. How many mystery books are children reading?

   ☐ _____
         label

Make Graphs and Interpret Data

► **Solve Problems Using a Bar Graph (continued)**

Animals at a Farm

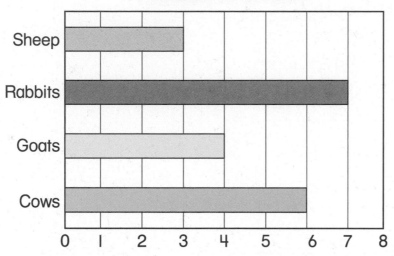

Use the bar graph to solve the problems.

Show your work.

6. The farm has 4 more rabbits than horses. How many horses does the farm have?

☐ _____
   label

7. The farm has 5 fewer goats than chickens. How many chickens does the farm have?

☐ _____
   label

8. There are 3 cows in the barn. The rest of the cows are in the field with the goats and the sheep. How many animals are in the field?

☐ _____
   label

▶ Solve *Compare* Problems with 2-Digit Numbers

Solve. Draw comparison bars for each.

---

9. A park has 46 maple trees. It has 18 fewer elm trees. How many elm trees are in the park?

    ☐ _____
       label

---

10. There are 62 pine trees in the park. There are 13 fewer pine trees than birch trees. How many birch trees are in the park?

    ☐ _____
       label

---

11. The park has 27 fir trees. There are 16 more spruce trees than fir trees. The park has 28 fewer spruce trees than oak trees. How many oak trees are in the park?

    ☐ _____
       label

Make Graphs and Interpret Data

Name

CA CC Content Standards 2.OA.1, 2.MD.10
Mathematical Practices MP.1, MP.4, MP.5, MP.6

► Math and Pets

Mrs. Pratt asks the children in her class to tell which
kitten they think is the cutest of these four kittens.

 Fluffy   Mink   Odin   Simba

The results of the survey are shown in this table.

Which Kitten Do You Think Is the Cutest?

Fluffy	○○○○○ ○
Mink	○○○○
Odin	○○○○○ ○○○○
Simba	○○○○○ ○

1. Use the information in the table to make a bar graph.

▶Take a Survey

Your teacher will ask all of the children in the class to tell which puppy they think is the cutest of these four puppies.

Romy   Parker   Domino   Bernie

Show the results of the survey in this table.

Which Puppy Do You Think Is the Cutest?

Romy	
Parker	
Domino	
Bernie	

2. Use the information in the table to make a bar graph on your MathBoard.

3. Write a 2-step word problem that can be solved by using the graph. Trade problems with a classmate. Solve each other's problems.

_____

_____

_____

Focus on Mathematical Practices

© Houghton Mifflin Harcourt Publishing Company • Image Credits: (tl) ©Life on white/Alamy Images; (tcl) ©GK Hart/Vikki Hart/PhotoDisc/Getty Images; (tcr) ©Life on white/PhotoDisc/Getty Images; (tr) ©Life on white/Alamy Images

Name _____

Use the table.

Roses Picked	
Brad	7
Mark	9
Pam	8
Luis	5

1. Make a picture graph to show the data in the table.

Title: _____

2. Make a bar graph to show the data in the table.

Title: _____

3. Use the picture graph. Choose the correct statements.

Strawberries								
Paula	🍓	🍓	🍓	🍓				
Reynaldo	🍓	🍓	🍓	🍓	🍓	🍓		

○ Paula has 2 more strawberries than Reynaldo.

○ Reynaldo has 2 more strawberries than Paula.

○ Paula and Reynaldo have 10 strawberries in all.

○ Reynaldo has 5 strawberries.

Use the bar graph to solve the problems.

4. The farm has 5 more goats than pigs. How many goats does the farm have?

☐ _____
label

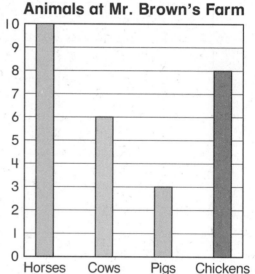

Animals at Mr. Brown's Farm

5. All of the horses and cows are in the pasture. Then 5 go back to the barn. Circle the number of animals that are still in the pasture.

10
11   animals are in the pasture.
16

6. If Mr. Brown's farm gets 3 more pigs, how many more horses than pigs will there be?

☐ _____
label

Use the bar graph.
Which statements are correct?
Choose Yes or No.

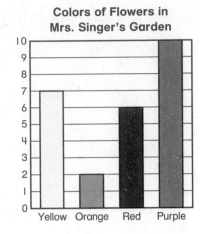

**Colors of Flowers in
Mrs. Singer's Garden**

7. There are 3 more purple flowers than
   yellow flowers.   ○ Yes   ○ No

8. There are 25 flowers in Mrs. Singer's
   garden in all.   ○ Yes   ○ No

9. If 4 of the yellow flowers are tulips and
   the rest are daffodils, there must be
   7 daffodils.   ○ Yes   ○ No

10. Mrs. Singer plants 6 more orange flowers
    in her garden. Now there are 2 more
    orange flowers than red flowers.   ○ Yes   ○ No

Circle the correct answer to complete the sentence.

11. At | 6:00 A.M. | Joel watches the sunrise.
       | 6:00 P.M. |

12. Owen has dinner at | 7:00 A.M. |
                       | 7:00 P.M. |

Write the correct number.

13. I hour = [   ] minutes   14. I day = [   ] hours

Write the time on each digital clock.

15.

16.

17.

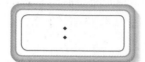

18. The football game starts at 1:40. Draw hands on the clock to show the time.

Mac arrives at the football field at 1:55. Does he see the start of the game? Explain how you know.

1:40

_____

_____

Solve. Draw comparison bars.

19. Elise picks 28 peaches. She picks 14 fewer than Charlie. How many peaches does Charlie pick?

[ ] _____

label

Dear Family:

In this unit, children will learn how to add 3-digit numbers that have totals up to 1,000.

Children begin the unit by learning to count to 1,000. They count by ones from a number, over the hundred, and into the next hundred. For example, 498, 499, 500, 501, 502, 503. You can help your child practice counting aloud to 1,000. Listen carefully as he or she crosses over the hundred.

Children will learn to write numbers to 1,000. Some children will write 5003 instead of 503 for five hundred three. Using Secret Code Cards will help children write the numbers correctly.

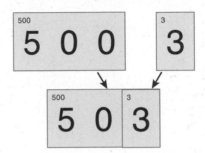

Help your child count small objects by making groups of 10 and then groups of 100. When the groups are made, help your child write the number of objects. This is a good way to help children recognize the difference between 5,003 and 503.

Please call if you have any questions or concerns. Thank you for helping your child learn about numbers to 1,000.

Sincerely,
Your child's teacher

© Houghton Mifflin Harcourt Publishing Company

CA CC

Unit 6 addresses the following standards from the *Common Core State Standards for Mathematics with California Additions*: **2.OA.1, 2.NBT.1, 2.NBT.1a, 2.NBT.1b, 2.NBT.2, 2.NBT.3, 2.NBT.4, 2.NBT.5, 2.NBT.7, 2.NBT.7.1, 2.NBT.8, 2.NBT.9, 2.MD.8,** and all Mathematical Practices.

Estimada familia:

En esta unidad los niños aprenderán cómo sumar números de 3 dígitos con totales de hasta 1,000.

Los niños comienzan la unidad aprendiendo a contar hasta 1,000. Cuentan de uno en uno a partir de un número, llegan a la centena y comienzan con la siguiente centena. Por ejemplo, 498, 499, 500, 501, 502, 503. Puede ayudar a su niño a practicar, contando en voz alta hasta 1,000. Ponga atención cada vez que llegue a una nueva centena.

Los niños aprenderán a escribir los números hasta 1,000. Tal vez, algunos niños escriban 5003 en vez de 503 al intentar escribir quinientos tres. Usar las Tarjetas de código secreto los ayudará a escribir correctamente los números.

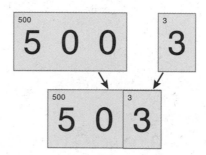

Ayude a su niño a contar objetos pequeños formando grupos de 10 y luego, grupos de 100. Cuando formen los grupos, ayúdelo a escribir el número de objetos. Esta es una buena manera de ayudar a los niños a reconocer la diferencia entre 5,003 y 503.

Si tiene alguna duda o pregunta, por favor comuníquese conmigo. Gracias por ayudar a su niño a aprender a contar hasta 1,000.

Atentamente,
El maestro de su niño

 CA CC

En la Unidad 6 se aplican los siguientes estándares auxiliares, contenidos en los *Estándares estatales comunes de matemáticas con adiciones para California*: **2.OA.1, 2.NBT.1, 2.NBT.1a, 2.NBT.1b, 2.NBT.2, 2.NBT.3, 2.NBT.4, 2.NBT.5, 2.NBT.7, 2.NBT.7.1, 2.NBT.8, 2.NBT.9, 2.MD.8** y todos los de prácticas matemáticas.

Name _____

CA CC Content Standards 2.NBT.1a, 2.NBT.1b, 2.NBT.2
Mathematical Practices MP.2, MP.5

► Count to 1,000 by Hundreds

Cut on dashed lines.

Dollars with Penny Array (back)

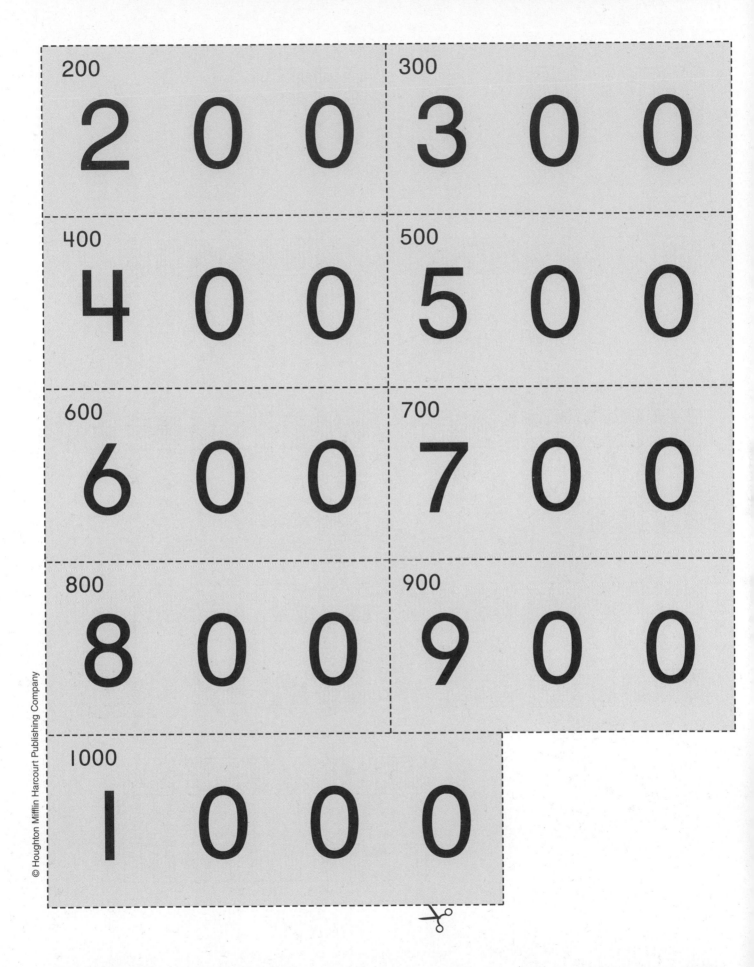

Secret Code Cards (200–1000)

Secret Code Cards (200–1000)

► Review the Use of Boxes, Sticks, and Circles to Represent Numbers

Write the number that is shown by the drawing.

1. ☐☐☐☐☐ ☐ ⫴⫴⫴ ⫴⫴

Total _____

_____   _____   _____

Hundreds   Tens   Ones

2. ☐☐☐ ⫴⫴ °°°°°

Total _____

_____   _____   _____

Hundreds   Tens   Ones

3. ☐☐☐☐ °°°°° °°°°

Total _____

_____   _____   _____

Hundreds   Tens   Ones

Draw boxes, sticks, and circles to show the number.

4. 740

_____

5. 876

_____

6. 294

_____

7. 502

▶ Expanded Form

Write the hundreds, tens, and ones.

8. 382 = _300_ + _80_ + _2_
   H T O

9. 738 = ____ + ____ + ____

10. 526 = ____ + ____ + ____

11. 267 = ____ + ____ + ____

Write the number.

12. 400 + 50 + 9 = _459_
                   H T O

13. 800 + 10 + 3 = ____

14. 100 + 70 + 5 = ____

15. 600 + 40 + 1 = ____

Write the number that makes the equation true.

16. ____ = 5 + 900 + 40

17. 7 + 200 = ____

18. ____ = 400 + 6 + 80

19. 800 + 40 = ____

20. ____ = 70 + 300

21. 60 + 500 + 3 = ____

22. ____ = 2 + 400

23. 9 + 90 + 200 = ____

24. 462 = 2 + 400 + ____

25. ____ + 90 + 700 = 798

26. 523 = 20 + 3 + ____

27. ____ + 4 + 200 = 224

Place Value

▶ Solve and Discuss

Write <, >, or =.

1. 635 ◯ 735

2. 527 ◯ 527

3. 820 ◯ 518

4. 327 ◯ 372

5. 975 ◯ 987

6. 321 ◯ 567

7. 267 ◯ 267

8. 271 ◯ 172

9. 654 ◯ 564

10. 750 ◯ 507

▶ What's the Error?

35 ⟩ 245

I know that 3 is greater than 2. Did I make a mistake?

11. Draw boxes, sticks, and circles to help Puzzled Penguin.

35 ◯ 245

▶ **Compare Numbers**

Write $<$, $>$, or $=$.

12. 620 ◯ 62

13. 510 ◯ 150

14. 852 ◯ 852

15. 854 ◯ 984

16. 71 ◯ 315

17. 357 ◯ 218

18. 418 ◯ 387

19. 482 ◯ 501

20. 359 ◯ 359

21. 376 ◯ 476

22. 291 ◯ 191

23. 333 ◯ 9

▶ **PATH to FLUENCY** **Add or Subtract Within 100**

Add.

24. $35 + 7 =$ _____

25. $6 + 77 =$ _____

26. $12 + 4 =$ _____

27. $\begin{array}{r} 19 \\ +60 \\ \hline \end{array}$

28. $\begin{array}{r} 35 \\ +42 \\ \hline \end{array}$

29. $\begin{array}{r} 27 \\ +73 \\ \hline \end{array}$

30. $\begin{array}{r} 58 \\ + 4 \\ \hline \end{array}$

Subtract.

31. $\begin{array}{r} 100 \\ -52 \\ \hline \end{array}$

32. $\begin{array}{r} 98 \\ -35 \\ \hline \end{array}$

33. $\begin{array}{r} 83 \\ -78 \\ \hline \end{array}$

34. $\begin{array}{r} 71 \\ -35 \\ \hline \end{array}$

© Houghton Mifflin Harcourt Publishing Company

Compare Numbers Within 999

► **Count Over a Hundred by Ones and by Tens**

Count by ones. Write the numbers.

1. 396   397   398   399   400   401   402   403   404

2. 594   595   ___   ___   ___   ___   ___   ___   602

3. 297   298   ___   ___   ___   ___   ___   ___   305

4. 495   ___   ___   ___   ___   ___   ___   ___   503

5. 598   ___   ___   ___   ___   ___   ___   ___   606

6. 697   ___   ___   ___   ___   ___   ___   ___   705

Count by tens. Write the numbers.

7. 460   470   480   490   500   510   520   530   540

8. 370   380   ___   ___   ___   ___   ___   ___   450

9. 640   650   ___   ___   ___   ___   ___   ___   720

10. 580   ___   ___   ___   ___   ___   ___   ___   660

11. 750   ___   ___   ___   ___   ___   ___   ___   830

12. 830   ___   ___   ___   ___   ___   ___   ___   910

Name _____

▶ Read and Write Number Names

You can write numbers with words or symbols.

1 one	11 eleven	10 ten	100 one hundred
2 two	12 twelve	20 twenty	200 two hundred
3 three	13 thirteen	30 thirty	300 three hundred
4 four	14 fourteen	40 forty	400 four hundred
5 five	15 fifteen	50 fifty	500 five hundred
6 six	16 sixteen	60 sixty	600 six hundred
7 seven	17 seventeen	70 seventy	700 seven hundred
8 eight	18 eighteen	80 eighty	800 eight hundred
9 nine	19 nineteen	90 ninety	900 nine hundred
			1,000 one thousand

Write each number.

13. one hundred twenty-five _____

14. four hundred fifty-eight _____

15. six hundred thirty-one _____

16. nine hundred sixty-two _____

17. eight hundred forty _____

18. seven hundred three _____

Write each number name.

19. 500 _____

20. 592 _____

21. 650 _____

22. 605 _____

23. 1,000 _____

Count by Ones and by Tens

Name _____

CA CC Content Standards 2.NBT.7, 2.NBT.9
Mathematical Practices MP.1, MP.3, MP.5, MP.6

▶ Add Numbers with 1, 2, and 3 Digits

Solve.

1. $200 + 200 = $ _____ $200 + 20 = $ _____ $200 + 2 = $ _____

   $300 + 300 = $ _____ $300 + 30 = $ _____ $300 + 3 = $ _____

   $400 + 400 = $ _____ $400 + 40 = $ _____ $400 + 4 = $ _____

   $500 + 500 = $ _____ $500 + 50 = $ _____ $500 + 5 = $ _____

2. $600 + 200 = $ _____ $20 + 600 = $ _____ $2 + 600 = $ _____

   $700 + 300 = $ _____ $30 + 700 = $ _____ $3 + 700 = $ _____

   $800 + 100 = $ _____ $10 + 800 = $ _____ $1 + 800 = $ _____

   $900 + 100 = $ _____ $10 + 900 = $ _____ $1 + 900 = $ _____

   $100 + 900 = $ _____ $90 + 100 = $ _____ $9 + 100 = $ _____

3. $100 + 134 = $ _____ $100 + 34 = $ _____ $4 + 100 = $ _____

   $200 + 245 = $ _____ $200 + 45 = $ _____ $200 + 5 = $ _____

   $300 + 356 = $ _____ $56 + 300 = $ _____ $6 + 300 = $ _____

   $400 + 467 = $ _____ $400 + 67 = $ _____ $400 + 7 = $ _____

   $500 + 478 = $ _____ $78 + 500 = $ _____ $8 + 500 = $ _____

▶ Solve and Discuss

Solve each word problem. Use Secret Code Cards
or draw proof drawings if you wish.

4. A camping club buys some
raisins. They buy 3 cartons
that have 100 bags each. They
also have 24 bags left from their
last trip. How many bags of
raisins does the club have?

□ _____
　　 label

5. Two friends want to make
necklaces. They buy 1 package
of one hundred red beads,
1 package of one hundred blue
beads, and 1 package of one
hundred green beads. They
already have 12 loose beads.
How many beads do they have
altogether?

□ _____
　　 label

6. Mia and Bo want to advertise
their yard sale. They decide
to make fliers. They buy
2 packs of paper. Each pack
has 200 sheets in it. They have
32 sheets in their art box.
How many sheets of paper
do they have?

□ _____
　　 label

7. All of the students at a school
go out on the playground. They
form 8 groups of one hundred
students and 6 groups of ten.
There are 5 students left.
How many students go to this
school?

□ _____
　　 label

Add Ones, Tens, and Hundreds

Dear Family:

Your child is now learning how to add 3-digit numbers. The methods children use are similar to those used for adding 2-digit numbers.

New Groups Below

Step 1	Step 2	Step 3
456	456	456
+ 278	+ 278	+ 278
4	34	734

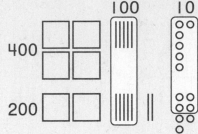

Children put the new 1 hundred or 1 ten on the line instead of at the top of the column. Many children find this less confusing because:

- They can see the 14.
- It is easier to add the 1 after they add the 5 and the 7.

Show All Totals

```
        456
      + 278
hundreds → 600
   tens → 120
   ones →  14
        734
```

Children see the hundreds, tens, and ones they are adding. These also can be seen when they make a math drawing like the one above.

Children may use any method that they understand, can explain, and can do fairly quickly. They should use hundreds, tens, and ones language to explain. This shows that they understand that they are adding 4 hundreds and 2 hundreds and not 4 and 2.

Please call if you have questions or comments.

Sincerely,
Your child's teacher

 CA CC

Unit 6 addresses the following standards from the *Common Core State Standards for Mathematics with California Additions*: **2.OA.1, 2.NBT.1, 2.NBT.1a, 2.NBT.1b, 2.NBT.2, 2.NBT.3, 2.NBT.4, 2.NBT.5, 2.NBT.7, 2.NBT.7.1, 2.NBT.8, 2.NBT.9, 2.MD.8,** and all Mathematical Practices.

Estimada familia:

Ahora su niño está aprendiendo a sumar números de 3 dígitos. Los métodos que los niños usarán son semejantes a los usados para sumar numeros de 2 dígitos.

Grupos nuevos abajo

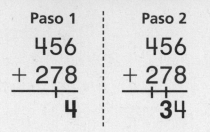

Paso 1	Paso 2	Paso 3
456	456	456
+ 278	+ 278	+ 278
4	34	734

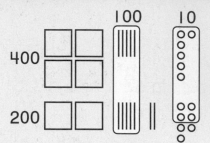

Los niños ponen la nueva centena o decena en la línea en vez de ponerla arriba de la columna. A muchos niños esto les resulta menos confuso porque:

- Pueden ver el 14.
- Es más fácil sumar el 1 después de que sumaron 5 y 7.

Mostrar todos los totales

456
+ 278

centenas ⟶ 600
decenas ⟶ 120
unidades ⟶ 14

734

Los niños ven las centenas, las decenas y las unidades que están sumando. Esto también se puede observar cuando hacen un dibujo matemático como el de arriba.

Los niños pueden usar cualquier método que comprendan, puedan explicar y puedan hacer relativamente rápido. Para explicar deben usar un lenguaje relacionado con centenas, decenas y unidades. Esto demuestra que entienden que están sumando 4 centenas y 2 centenas, y no 4 y 2.

Si tiene alguna duda o pregunta, por favor comuníquese conmigo.

Atentamente,
El maestro de su niño

CA CC

En la Unidad 6 se aplican los siguientes estándares auxiliares, contenidos en los *Estándares estatales comunes de matemáticas con adiciones para California*: **2.OA.1, 2.NBT.1, 2.NBT.1a, 2.NBT.1b, 2.NBT.2, 2.NBT.3, 2.NBT.4, 2.NBT.5, 2.NBT.7, 2.NBT.7.1, 2.NBT.8, 2.NBT.9, 2.MD.8** y todos los de prácticas matemáticas.

© Houghton Mifflin Harcourt Publishing Company

► **Solve and Discuss**

Solve each word problem.
Be ready to explain what you did.

1. Milo makes a display of plant
   and fish fossils for the library.
   He puts in 478 plant fossils. He
   puts in 67 fish fossils. How many
   fossils are in the display?

   ▭ _____
        label

2. The nature club plants some
   pine and birch trees. They plant
   496 birch trees. Then they plant
   283 pine trees. How many trees
   does the club plant in all?

   ▭ _____
        label

3. There are 818 ducks entered
   in the Rubber Duck River Race.
   Then 182 more are added.
   How many ducks are in
   the race now?

   ▭ _____
        label

4. There are 189 children at
   Camp Sunshine. There are 375
   children at Camp Bluebird. How
   many children are there at the
   two camps?

   ▭ _____
        label

▶ Practice 3-Digit Addition

Add using any method. Make a proof drawing if it helps.

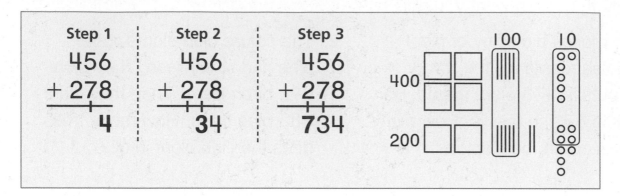

Step 1	Step 2	Step 3
456	456	456
+278	+278	+278
4	34	734

5. 375
   +482

6. 148
   +236

7. 584
   + 61

8. 168
   +674

9.   89
   +376

10. 563
    +157

11. 497
    +259

12. 124
    +563

13. 348
    +239

3-Digit Addition

Name _____

CA CC Content Standards 2.NBT.7, 2.NBT.9
Mathematical Practices MP.3, MP.5, MP.6, MP.8

▶ New Ten or New Hundred

Add. Use any method. Make a proof drawing if it helps.

1.
```
   2 3 6
 + 4 7 8
 _____
```

Make a new ten? _____

Make a new hundred? _____

2. $183 + 517 =$ _____

Make a new ten? _____

Make a new hundred? _____

3. $93 + 485 =$ _____

Make a new ten? _____

Make a new hundred? _____

4.
```
   3 6 8
 + 2 5 7
 _____
```

Make a new ten? _____

Make a new hundred? _____

5. $347 + 37 =$ _____

Make a new ten? _____

Make a new hundred? _____

6. $645 + 87 =$ _____

Make a new ten? _____

Make a new hundred? _____

Discuss 3-Digit Addition **277**

Name _____

▶New Ten, New Hundred, or New Thousand

Add. Use any method. Draw a proof drawing if it helps.

7.
```
   195
 +172
```

Make a new ten? _____

Make a new hundred? _____

Make a new thousand? _____

8.
```
   300
 +700
```

Make a new ten? _____

Make a new hundred? _____

Make a new thousand? _____

9. $360 + 640 =$ _____

Make a new ten? _____

Make a new hundred? _____

Make a new thousand? _____

10. $75 + 823 =$ _____

Make a new ten? _____

Make a new hundred? _____

Make a new thousand? _____

11. $905 + 95 =$ _____

Make a new ten? _____

Make a new hundred? _____

Make a new thousand? _____

12. $413 + 587 =$ _____

Make a new ten? _____

Make a new hundred? _____

Make a new thousand? _____

Discuss 3-Digit Addition

▶ Find the Hidden Animal

Directions for the puzzle on page 280.

1. Start by coloring in the six dotted squares. These are "free" squares. They are part of the puzzle solution.

2. Find one of the sums below. Then look for that sum in the puzzle grid. Color in that puzzle piece.

3. Find all 20 sums. Color the puzzle pieces with the sums. Color in all 20 correct answers.

4. Name the hidden animal. It is a(n) _____.

524	287	384	456	327
+247	+164	+375	+174	+265

207	248	282	548	233
+595	+376	+457	+387	+288

367	293	284	537	138
+265	+595	+376	+463	+327

286	407	503	78	192
+ 78	+266	+148	+65	+339

See page 279 for directions on how to solve the puzzle.

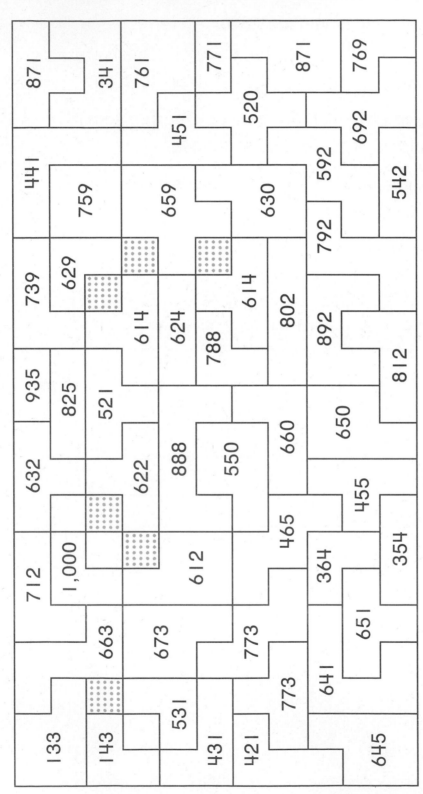

Discuss 3-Digit Addition

▶ Adding Up to Solve Word Problems

Solve each word problem.

Show your work.

1. Mr. Cruz has 750 yams to sell. He sells
   some and has 278 yams left. How many
   yams does he sell?

   ☐ _____
   label

2. At the end of February there are 692 houses
   in our town. Some new houses are built in
   March. At the end of March there are 976
   houses. How many houses are built in March?

   ☐ _____
   label

3. Delia has 524 rocks in her collection. She
   gives some to her sister. Now she has 462
   rocks. How many rocks did she give away?

   ☐ _____
   label

4. On Saturday, 703 people go to a movie.
   194 go in the afternoon. The rest go in
   the evening. How many people go in the
   evening?

   ☐ _____
   label

► Adding Up to Solve Word Problems (continued)

Solve each word problem.   **Show your work.**

5. Jeremy makes 525 coasters that are circles or squares as gifts for his family. 347 coasters are circles. How many coasters are squares?

   [_____] _____
                    label

6. Analisse has 419 marbles. 287 of the marbles are blue. How many marbles are other colors?

   [_____] _____
                    label

► PATH to FLUENCY Add and Subtract Within 100

Add.

7. 32	8. 42	9. 57	10. 44
+ 50	+ 57	+ 43	+ 7

Subtract.

11. 98	12. 100	13. 43	14. 61
− 24	− 31	− 38	− 29

Word Problems: Unknown Addends

Family Letter
Content Overview

Dear Family:

Your child is now learning how to subtract 3-digit numbers. The most important part is understanding and being able to explain a method. Children may use any method that they understand, can explain, and can perform fairly quickly.

Expanded Method	Ungroup First Method

Expanded Method

Step 1   **Step 2**

$$
\begin{aligned}
& \quad\quad\quad\quad\quad 120 \\
& \quad\quad\quad\quad 300 \;\; \cancel{20} \;\; 12 \\
432 &= 400 + 30 + 2 = \cancel{400} + \cancel{30} + \cancel{2} \\
-273 &= 200 + 70 + 3 = 200 + 70 + 3
\end{aligned}
$$

Step 3 $\begin{cases} 100 + 50 + 9 \\ = 159 \end{cases}$

Step 1 "Expand" each number to show that it is made up of hundreds, tens, and ones.

Step 2 Check to see if there are enough ones to subtract from. If not, ungroup a ten into 10 ones and add it to the existing ones. Check to see if there are enough tens to subtract from. If not, ungroup a hundred into 10 tens and add it to the existing tens. Children may also ungroup from the left.

Step 3 Subtract to find the answer. Children may subtract from left to right or right to left.

Ungroup First Method

Step 1 Check to see if there are enough ones and tens to subtract from. Ungroup where needed.

Look inside 432. Ungroup 432 and rename it as 3 hundreds, 12 tens, and 12 ones.

Ungroup from the left: **Ungroup from the right:**

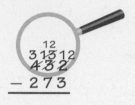   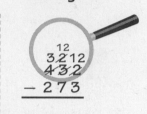

Step 2 Subtract to find the answer. Children may subtract from the left or from the right.

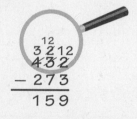

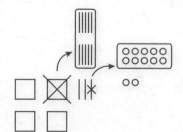

In explaining any method they use, children are expected to use "hundreds, tens, and ones" language and drawings to show that they understand place value.

Please call if you have questions or comments.

Sincerely,
Your child's teacher

 CA CC

Unit 6 addresses the following standards from the *Common Core State Standards for Mathematics with California Additions*: **2.OA.1, 2.NBT.1, 2.NBT.1a, 2.NBT.1b, 2.NBT.2, 2.NBT.3, 2.NBT.4, 2.NBT.7, 2.NBT.7.1, 2.NBT.8, 2.NBT.9, 2.MD.8**, and all Mathematical Practices.

Estimada familia:

Su niño está aprendiendo a restar números de 3 dígitos. Lo más importante es comprender y saber explicar un método. Los niños pueden usar cualquier método que comprendan, puedan explicar y puedan hacer relativamente rápido.

Método extendido	**Método de desagrupar primero**

Método extendido

Paso 1   **Paso 2**

$$432 = 400 + 30 + 2 = \overset{300}{\cancel{400}} + \overset{\overset{120}{20}}{\cancel{30}} + \overset{12}{\cancel{2}}$$
$$- 273 = 200 + 70 + 3 = 200 + 70 + 3$$

Paso 3 $\begin{cases} 100 + 50 + 9 \\ = 159 \end{cases}$

Paso 1 "Extender" cada número para mostrar que consta de centenas, decenas y unidades.

Paso 2 Observar si hay suficientes unidades para restar. Si no, desagrupar una decena para formar 10 unidades y sumarlas a las unidades existentes. Observar si hay suficientes decenas para restar. Si no, desagrupar una centena para formar 10 decenas y sumarlas a las decenas existentes. Los niños también pueden desagrupar por la izquierda.

Paso 3 Restar para hallar la respuesta. Los niños pueden restar de izquierda a derecha o de derecha a izquierda.

Método de desagrupar primero

Paso 1 Observar si hay suficientes unidades y decenas para restar. Desagrupar cuando haga falta.

Mirar dentro de 432. Desagrupar 432 y volver a nombrarlo como 3 centenas, 12 decenas y 12 unidades.

Desagrupar por la izquierda: **Desagrupar por la derecha:**

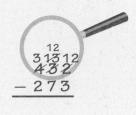   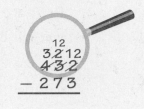

Paso 2 Restar para hallar la respuesta. Los niños pueden restar empezando por la izquierda o por la derecha.

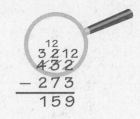

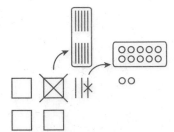

Para explicar cualquier método que usen, los niños deben usar lenguaje y dibujos relacionados con centenas, decenas y unidades para demostrar que comprenden el valor posicional.

Si tiene alguna duda o comentario, por favor comuníquese conmigo.

Atentamente,
El maestro de su niño

CA CC

En la Unidad 6 se aplican los siguientes estándares auxiliares, contenidos en los *Estándares estatales comunes de matemáticas con adiciones para California*: 2.OA.1, 2.NBT.1, 2.NBT.1a, 2.NBT.1b, 2.NBT.2, 2.NBT.3, 2.NBT.4, 2.NBT.5, 2.NBT.7, 2.NBT.7.1, 2.NBT.8, 2.NBT.9, 2.MD.8 y todos los de prácticas matemáticas.

Subtract from Hundreds Numbers

▶ Discuss Subtraction Problems

Solve each word problem. Use any method.
Make a proof drawing.

1. A teacher buys 200 erasers for his students. He gives 152 of them away. How many erasers does he have left over?

   □□□ _____
   label

2. The school cafeteria has 500 apples. Some of them are served with lunch. After lunch, there are 239 apples left. How many apples does the cafeteria serve?

   □□□ _____
   label

3. Teresa sells guitars. She has 600 guitars. She sells 359. How many guitars does she have left?

   □□□ _____
   label

4. Jorge is on a basketball team. He scores 181 points one year. He scores some points in a second year, too. He scores a total of 400 points over the two years. How many points does he score the second year?

   □□□ _____
   label

▶ Practice Subtracting from 1,000

Subtract. Use any method.

5.
```
   1,000
 −   772
```

6.
```
   1,000
 −   526
```

7.
```
   1,000
 −   843
```

8.
```
   1,000
 −   293
```

9.
```
   1,000
 −    95
```

10.
```
   1,000
 −   157
```

11. Elliot has 1,000 pennies. He puts 350 pennies in penny rolls. How many pennies are left?

12. Marta's class plans to collect 1,000 cans this year. They have 452 cans so far. How many more cans do they plan to collect?

label

label

6-10

Class Activity

Name _____

CA CC Content Standards 2.NBT.5, 2.NBT.7, 2.NBT.9
Mathematical Practices MP.1, MP.2, MP.5, MP.6

VOCABULARY
ungroup

▶ Do I Need to Ungroup?

Decide if you need to **ungroup**. If you need to ungroup, draw a magnifying glass around the top number. Then find the answer.

1.
```
  508
- 346
```

Ungroup to get 10 ones? _____

Ungroup to get 10 tens? _____

2.
```
  500
- 306
```

Ungroup to get 10 ones? _____

Ungroup to get 10 tens? _____

3.
```
  670
- 340
```

Ungroup to get 10 ones? _____

Ungroup to get 10 tens? _____

4.
```
  570
- 390
```

Ungroup to get 10 ones? _____

Ungroup to get 10 tens? _____

Name _____

▶ Subtract from 3-Digit Numbers with Zeros

Subtract.

5. 4 0 6
    − 1 8 1

6. 7 9 0
    − 2 7 2

7. 3 4 0
    − 1 1 8

8. 5 0 7
    − 4 3 8

9. 4 0 0
    − 2 6 3

10. 5 0 0
    − 2 3 4

▶ PATH to FLUENCY Add and Subtract Within 100

Add.

11. 3 8
    + 4 4

12. 6 1
    + 1 7

13. 3 6
    + 6 4

14. 7 8
    + 1 9

Subtract.

15. 1 0 0
    − 5 7

16. 9 2
    − 4 0

17. 6 4
    − 2 5

18. 8 1
    − 1 9

Subtract from Numbers with Zeros

VOCABULARY
estimate
round

▶ Round to the Nearest Hundred

Round 268 to the nearest hundred. Follow these steps:

Step 1: Underline the number in the hundreds' place. **268**

Step 2: Write the hundred that is greater than 268 above
and write the hundred that is less than 268 below.

Step 3: Make a drawing to show each number.

Step 4: If there are 5 or more <u>tens</u>, round up.
If there are less than 5 <u>tens</u>, round down.

300 ☐ ☐ ☐

268 ☐ ☐ |||||| ○○○○○ ○○○○

6 is 5 or more,
so round up.

200 ☐ ☐

▶ Practice Rounding

Round the number to the nearest hundred. You may use drawings.

1. 112 ☐

2. 283 ☐

3. 242 ☐

4. 439 ☐

5. 664 ☐

6. 553 ☐

▶ Round to Estimate Answers

Round each number to the nearest hundred.
Then add or subtract the rounded numbers.
Circle the answer that is the better estimate.

7. $\begin{array}{r} 2\,1\,4 \\ +\,1\,2\,4 \\ \hline \end{array}$ 8. $\begin{array}{r} 3\,8\,0 \\ +\,2\,3\,4 \\ \hline \end{array}$ 9. $\begin{array}{r} 4\,6\,6 \\ +\,1\,7\,7 \\ \hline \end{array}$

200 or 300   600 or 800   600 or 700

10. $\begin{array}{r} 6\,2\,3 \\ -\,2\,2\,1 \\ \hline \end{array}$ 11. $\begin{array}{r} 8\,6\,1 \\ -\,3\,7\,4 \\ \hline \end{array}$ 12. $\begin{array}{r} 4\,8\,4 \\ -\,2\,3\,7 \\ \hline \end{array}$

400 or 500   400 or 500   200 or 300

▶ Solve by rounding.   Show your work.

13. Warren scored 411 points in the first game
    and 385 points in the second game. Round
    each number to the nearest hundred. *About*
    how many points did Warren score altogether?

    about [　　　] _____
                          label

14. Robin had 630 coins in her collection. She
    gave 198 coins to her brother. Round each
    number to the nearest hundred. *About* how
    many coins does Robin have now?

    about [　　　] _____
                          label

Practice Ungrouping

► Review Addition and Subtraction

Ring *add* or *subtract*. Check if you need to ungroup or make a new ten or hundred. Then find the answer.

1.
$$762$$
$$-395$$

Subtract

☐ Ungroup to get 10 ones

☐ Ungroup to get 10 tens

Add

☐ Make 1 new ten

☐ Make 1 new hundred

2.
$$395$$
$$+367$$

Subtract

☐ Ungroup to get 10 ones

☐ Ungroup to get 10 tens

Add

☐ Make 1 new ten

☐ Make 1 new hundred

3.
$$287$$
$$-193$$

Subtract

☐ Ungroup to get 10 ones

☐ Ungroup to get 10 tens

Add

☐ Make 1 new ten

☐ Make 1 new hundred

4.
$$437$$
$$+324$$

Subtract

☐ Ungroup to get 10 ones

☐ Ungroup to get 10 tens

Add

☐ Make 1 new ten

☐ Make 1 new hundred

VOCABULARY
opposite operation

▶ Relate Addition and Subtraction

Decide whether you need to add or subtract.
Draw a Math Mountain. Check your answer by using
the **opposite operation**.

5. $\begin{array}{r} 5\,3\,2 \\ -1\,8\,1 \\ \hline \end{array}$ ✓

6. $\begin{array}{r} 5\,3\,2 \\ +1\,8\,1 \\ \hline \end{array}$ ✓

7. $\begin{array}{r} 5\,2\,8 \\ +3\,5\,7 \\ \hline \end{array}$ ✓

8. $\begin{array}{r} 1{,}0\,0\,0 \\ -\ \ 4\,3\,8 \\ \hline \end{array}$ ✓

9. $\begin{array}{r} 5\,7\,1 \\ +2\,8\,7 \\ \hline \end{array}$ ✓

10. $\begin{array}{r} 9\,0\,4 \\ -4\,5\,8 \\ \hline \end{array}$ ✓

Relationships Between Addition and Subtraction Methods

▶ Solve and Discuss

Make a drawing. Write an equation.
Solve the problem.

1. Lucero spills a bag of marbles. 219 fall on the floor. 316 are still in the bag. How many were in the bag in the beginning?

[ ] _____
label

2. Al counts bugs in the park. He counts 561 on Monday. He counts 273 fewer than that on Tuesday. How many bugs does he count on Tuesday?

[ ] _____
label

3. Happy the Clown gives out balloons. She gives out 285 at the zoo and then she gives out some more at the amusement park. Altogether she gives out 503. How many balloons does she give out at the amusement park?

[ ] _____
label

4. Charlie the Clown gives out 842 balloons at the fun fair. He gives out 194 at the store. He gives out 367 at the playground. How many more balloons does he give out at the fun fair than at the playground?

[ ] _____
label

▶ Solve and Discuss (continued)

Make a drawing. Write an equation. Solve the problem.

5. Damon collects stamps. He has 383 stamps. Then he buys 126 more at a yard sale. How many stamps does he have now?

[ ] _____
        label

6. Mr. Lewis sells 438 melons. Now he has 294 melons left. How many melons did he have at the start?

[ ] _____
        label

7. Ali is giving out ribbons for a race. She gave out 57 ribbons so far, and she has 349 ribbons left. How many ribbons did she have at the start?

[ ] _____
        label

8. Cora collected 542 sports cards last year. She collected 247 fewer than that this year. How many cards did she collect in both years together?

[ ] _____
        label

Mixed Addition and Subtraction Word Problems

▶ Solve and Discuss (continued)

Make a drawing. Write an equation. Solve the problem.

9. Tanya is working on a puzzle. She has placed 643 pieces. There are 1,000 pieces in the puzzle. How many more pieces does she have to place?

[ ] _____
    label

10. In March the Shaws plant some flowers. In April they plant 178 more flowers. In the two months they plant a total of 510 flowers. How many flowers do they plant in March?

[ ] _____
    label

11. Jeremy has 48 action figures. Jeremy has 14 more action figures than Keith. How many action figures does Keith have?

[ ] _____
    label

12. Pawel gives out fliers about a play. He gives out 194 fliers at the bakery. He gives out 358 at the grocery store. How many fewer fliers does he give out at the bakery than at the grocery store?

[ ] _____
    label

▶ **Solve and Discuss (continued)**

Make a drawing. Write an equation. Solve the problem.

13. Rue has 842 buttons. Then she gives some to a friend. Now she has 263 buttons. How many buttons does Rue give to her friend?

```
┌──────┐
│      │  _____
└──────┘       label
```

14. Last week Jan sold some tickets to a play. She sells 345 more this week. Altogether she sells 500 tickets. How many tickets did she sell last week?

```
┌──────┐
│      │  _____
└──────┘       label
```

15. April has 98 fewer pennies than Julie has. April has 521 pennies. How many pennies does Julie have?

```
┌──────┐
│      │  _____
└──────┘       label
```

16. There are 675 plastic cups and 300 paper plates in a cabinet. Jaime puts more cups and plates in the cabinet. Now there are 850 cups. How many cups does Jaime add?

```
┌──────┐
│      │  _____
└──────┘       label
```

▶ Math and Artists

Many artists sell their work at art fairs.

Solve.

1. On one weekend, 489 people come to the art fair on Saturday and 511 people come to the fair on Sunday. How many people come to the fair in all?

    ☐ _____
         label

2. Wendy uses silver and blue beads to make necklaces to sell. She uses 72 blue beads. She uses 38 more blue beads than silver beads. How many silver beads does she use?

    ☐ _____
         label

3. LeBron uses tiny seed beads to make bracelets. He buys a package of seed beads with 350 red beads and 250 white beads. After he makes the bracelets for the fair, he has just 6 beads left. How many beads does he use?

    ☐ _____
         label

▶ **Caricatures**

A caricature is a drawing of a person.
The drawing looks like a cartoon.

- Last week, an artist drew
  146 children and 84 adults.

- This week, the artist drew
  167 children and 55 adults.

Solve. Use the information in the box above.

4. How many people did the artist draw last week?

☐ _____
         label

5. How many people did the artist draw this week?

☐ _____
         label

6. How many fewer people did the artist draw
   this week than last week?

☐ _____
         label

7. Did the artist draw more children or more adults?

more _____

Focus on Mathematical Practices

1. Write the number that is shown by the drawing.

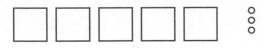

_____   _____   _____   _____
Hundreds   Tens   Ones   Total

___

2. Ming has some baseball cards. He gives 210 of them away. Now he has 323 cards. How many baseball cards did Ming have to start? Circle the number to complete the sentence.

Ming had | 113
          | 503 | cards to start.
          | 533

___

3. Is this a way to show 613? Choose Yes or No.

6 + 1 + 3	○ Yes	○ No
600 + 10 + 3	○ Yes	○ No
six hundred thirty-one	○ Yes	○ No
six hundred thirteen	○ Yes	○ No

___

4. Claudia has 36 rocks in her collection. She has 49 fewer rocks than Luisa. How many rocks does Luisa have in her collection?

Show your work.

☐ _____
          label

5. Choose the ways that show counting by 10s.

○ 430   431   432   433   434   435   436   437

○ 260   270   280   290   300   310   320   330

○ 200   300   400   500   600   700   800   900

○ 510   520   530   540   550   560   570   580

○ 930   940   950   960   970   980   990   1,000

6. Count by 100s. Write the numbers.

300   400   _____ _____ _____ _____ _____ _____

7. The Nature Club made a 4 page flier of nature photos. They want to print 100 copies of the flier. They have 258 sheets of paper. They buy a pack of 200 sheets. Do they have enough paper to print the fliers? Explain.

_____

_____

_____

The club adds one more page of photos to each flier. Do they have enough paper to print them now? Explain.

_____

_____

8. Match the numbers to <, =, or >.

461 ◯ 416 •   • =

324 ◯ 324 •   • <

692 ◯ 902 •   • >

9. On Tuesday, 222 books are returned to the
   library. 387 books are returned on Wednesday.
   Round each number to the nearest hundred. *About*
   how many books are returned to the library?

   about [＿＿＿] ＿＿＿＿＿＿＿＿
                      label

10. Add. Then choose Yes or No about what you did.

    574
    + 326
    ＿＿＿

    Make a new ten?   ◯ Yes   ◯ No
    Make a new hundred?   ◯ Yes   ◯ No
    Make a new thousand?   ◯ Yes   ◯ No

11. Samira has 285 beads. 96 of them are red. The   **Show your work.**
    rest of the beads are blue. How many blue beads
    does Samira have?

    [＿＿＿] ＿＿＿＿＿＿＿＿
                 label

Solve.

12. 596 − 100 = _____

13. 603 − 10 = _____

---

14. Ada read 124 pages in a book. The book has
300 pages. How many more pages does she
still have to read to finish the book?
Make a drawing. Write an equation. Solve the problem.

_____
label

---

15. Show and explain how to subtract 279 from 458.
Use the words *hundreds, tens,* and *ones.* Explain
how and why you can use addition to check your
answer.

_____

_____

_____

_____

_____

Dear Family:

In this unit, your child will learn about rectangular arrays and how to use addition to count the number of objects in an array. The array below has 2 rows and 3 columns. It can be described as 2 rows with 3 tiles in each row or 3 columns with 2 tiles in each column.

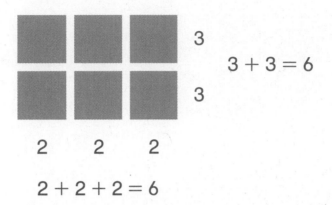

You can help your child by working with him or her to practice using the words *array*, *rows*, and *columns*. For example, ask your child to use pennies or other small objects to make an array that has 4 rows with 5 objects in each row. Ask your child to write the addition equations that show the total number of objects in the array. ($5 + 5 + 5 + 5 = 20$ and $4 + 4 + 4 + 4 + 4 = 20$)

Your child will also be learning about equal parts of circles and rectangles: 2 *halves*, 3 *thirds*, and 4 *fourths*. You can practice using this vocabulary at home. For example, "I am cutting this pizza into 4 fourths."

Please call if you have any questions or concerns.

Sincerely,
Your child's teacher

 CA CC

Unit 7 addresses the following standards from the *Common Core State Standards for Mathematics with California Additions*: 2.OA.1, 2.OA.3, 2.OA.4, 2.NBT.5, 2.NBT.6, 2.MD.1, 2.MD.5, 2.MD.6, 2.G.1, 2.G.2, 2.G.3, and all Mathematical Practices.

Estimada familia:

En esta unidad, su niño aprenderá acerca de las matrices rectangulares y aprenderá cómo usar la suma para contar el número de objetos en una matriz. La matriz de abajo tiene 2 hileras y 3 columnas. Puede describirse así: 2 hileras con 3 fichas en cada columna, o 3 columnas con 2 fichas en cada columna.

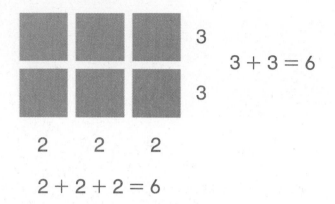

$$3 + 3 = 6$$

$$2 + 2 + 2 = 6$$

Usted puede ayudar a su niño practicando el uso de las palabras *matriz, hileras* y *columnas.* Por ejemplo, pídale que use monedas de un centavo u otros objetos pequeños para hacer una matriz que tenga 4 hileras con 5 objetos en cada una. Pida a su niño que escriba la ecuación de suma que muestra el número total de objetos en la matriz. ($5 + 5 + 5 + 5 = 20$ y $4 + 4 + 4 + 4 + 4 = 20$)

Su niño también aprenderá acerca de partes iguales de círculos y rectángulos: 2 *medios,* 3 *tercios* y 4 *cuartos.* Pueden practicar usando este vocabulario en casa. Por ejemplo: "Estoy cortando esta pizza en 4 cuartos".

Si tiene alguna duda o algún comentario, por favor comuníquese conmigo.

Atentamente,
El maestro de su niño

© Houghton Mifflin Harcourt Publishing Company

CA CC

En la Unidad 7 se aplican los siguientes estándares auxiliares, contenidos en los *Estándares estatales comunes de matemáticas con adiciones para California:* 2.OA.1, 2.OA.3, 2.OA.4, 2.NBT.5, 2.NBT.6, 2.MD.1, 2.MD.5, 2.MD.6, 2.G.1, 2.G.2, 2.G.3 y todos los de prácticas matemáticas.

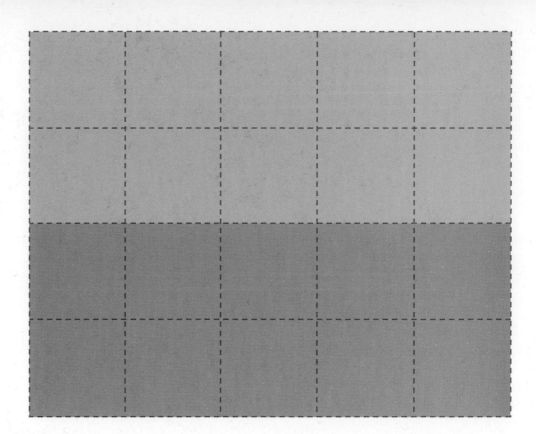

Square-Inch Tiles

CA CC Content Standards 2.OA.3, 2.OA.4, 2.MD.1, 2.G.1, 2.G.2, 2.G.3 Mathematical Practices MP.2, MP.5, MP.6, MP.8

VOCABULARY
array
rows
columns

▶ Rows and Columns

1. Loop the **rows**.

2. Loop the **columns**.

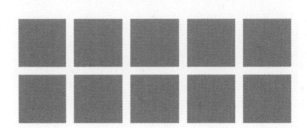

▶ Write Equations for Arrays

Write how many in each row and in each column.
Then write two equations for each **array**.

3.

  _____

  _____

  _____

_____ _____

_____

_____

4.

 _____

  _____

_____ _____ _____ _____

_____

_____

► Measure to Partition Rectangles

Measure in inches. Draw rows and columns.
Write the number of small squares.

5.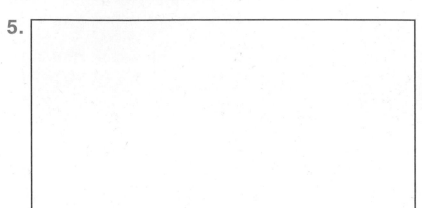

_____ squares

6.

_____ squares

Measure in centimeters. Draw rows and columns.
Write the number of small squares.

7.

_____ squares

8.

_____ squares

9.

_____ squares

VOCABULARY
halves
thirds
fourths

▶ Shade Equal Shares

Measure in centimeters. Draw rows and columns.
Shade to show **halves**, **thirds**, and **fourths**.

10. halves

11. thirds

12. fourths

Measure in centimeters. Draw rows and columns.

13. Shade to show halves two different ways.

14. Shade to show fourths two different ways.

15. Shade to show halves two different ways.

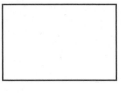

Name _____

▶ More Practice with Partitions and Equal Shares

Measure in centimeters. Draw rows and columns.
Write the number of small squares.

16.

17.

18.

_____ squares   _____ squares   _____ squares

19.

20.

21.

_____ squares   _____ squares   _____ squares

Shade to show **equal shares**.

22. 2 halves

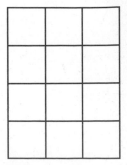

23. 3 thirds

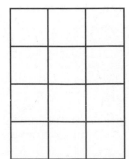

24. 4 fourths

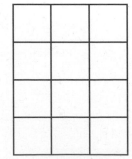

Arrays, Partitioned Rectangles, and Equal Shares

► Different Shapes of a Half of the Same Rectangle

1. Make two halves. Show different ways.
   Shade half of each rectangle.

► Different Shapes of a Third of the Same Rectangle

2. Make three thirds. Show different ways.
   Shade a third of each rectangle.

► Different Shapes of a Fourth of the Same Rectangle

3. Make four fourths. Show different ways.
   Shade a fourth of each rectangle.

▶ Equal Shares Using the Same Square

4. Make 2 equal shares. Show different ways. Shade half of each square.

5. Make 3 equal shares. Show different ways. Shade a third of each square.

6. Make 4 equal shares. Show different ways. Shade a fourth of each square.

▶ Equal Shares Using the Same Circle

7. Make 2 equal shares. Shade half of the circle.

8. Make 3 equal shares. Shade a third of the circle.

9. Make 4 equal shares. Shade a fourth of the circle.

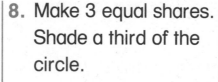

▶ Different Shape but Same Size

10. Use Drawings 1, 2, and 3 to explain why the blue and yellow shares are equal.

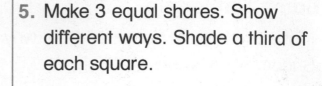

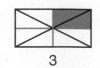

1   2   3

► **Solve and Discuss**

Solve.   **Show your work.**

1. Carl draws a line segment that is 18 centimeters long.
   Then he makes it 14 centimeters longer. How long
   is the line segment now?

   ☐ _____
              unit

2. Samantha runs 45 meters, stops, and then she runs
   some more. She runs a total of 95 meters. How many
   meters does she run after her stop?

   ☐ _____
              unit

3. A ribbon is 48 inches long. Taylor uses 32 inches of
   the ribbon to make a bow. How much ribbon is left?

   ☐ _____
              unit

4. Mr. Parker cut 9 feet from the end of a pole. The pole
   is now 22 feet long. How long was the pole before
   Mr. Parker cut it?

   ☐ _____
              unit

▶ Solve and Discuss (continued)

Solve.

Show your work.

5. A race course is 99 meters long. There are trees along 38 meters of the course. How long is the part of the course without trees?

□ _____
unit

6. Michelle paints a fence that is 81 feet long. Huck paints a fence that is 56 feet long. How much longer is the fence Michelle paints?

□ _____
unit

7. O'Shanti has a necklace that is 24 centimeters long. She makes the necklace 36 centimeters longer. How long is the necklace now?

□ _____
unit

8. A giant flag is 6 meters long. Vern adds 4 meters to its length. How long is the flag now?

□ _____
unit

▶ Solve and Discuss (continued)

Solve.   **Show your work.**

---

9. Kelly has a piece of red yarn that is 25 centimeters long. She also has a piece of blue yarn that is 11 centimeters long. How much longer is the red yarn than the blue yarn?

```
┌──────┐
│      │  _____
└──────┘       unit
```

---

10. Paco swims 41 meters. Kenny swims 4 meters less than Paco. How far does Kenny swim?

```
┌──────┐
│      │  _____
└──────┘       unit
```

---

11. Leonard walks 28 meters. Then he walks 56 more meters. How many meters does he walk in all?

```
┌──────┐
│      │  _____
└──────┘       unit
```

---

12. A tree is 72 inches tall now. It is 12 inches taller than it was last year. How tall was the tree last year?

```
┌──────┐
│      │  _____
└──────┘       unit
```

► Number Line Diagrams

Use the number line diagram to add or subtract.

---

13. Loop 17 and 28. Loop the difference *D*.

How long is it? _____

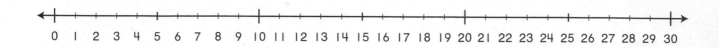

---

14. Loop 17 and 35. Loop the difference *D*.

How long is it? _____

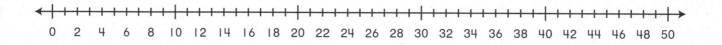

---

15. Loop 38 and 84. Loop the difference *D*.

How long is it? _____

---

16. Loop 67. Add 26 to it. Loop the total *T*.

How long is it? _____

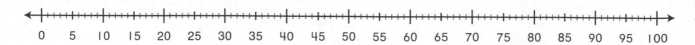

▶ Lengths at the Grocery Store

Choose a method to solve the problems. Does your
method work for all of them? Be ready to explain your
method to the class.

1. Someone breaks a jug of milk in
   the store. Mr. Green cleans it up.
   Then he blocks off the wet spot
   with tape. How long is the tape?

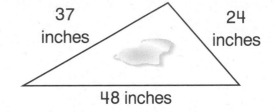

37 inches   24 inches

48 inches

_____ unit

2. Mrs. Chang wants to decorate
   the table she uses for free food
   samples. She wants to put gold
   trim around the top of the table.
   How much trim will she need?

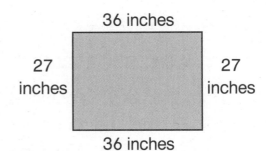

36 inches

27 inches   27 inches

36 inches

_____ unit

3. Here is the route a customer
   takes while shopping at the store.
   How far does the customer walk
   altogether?

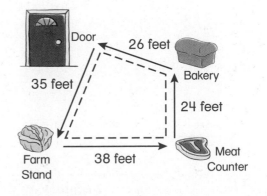

Door   26 feet

35 feet   Bakery

24 feet

Farm   38 feet   Meat
Stand   Counter

_____ unit

© Houghton Mifflin Harcourt Publishing Company

▶Playground Lengths

Solve.   **Show your work.**

---

4. The basketball court has sides that are 42 feet, 37 feet, 42 feet, and 37 feet and four right angles. What is the distance around the court?

[_____] _____
                unit

5. The fence around the picnic area has sides with lengths of 33 yards, 56 yards, and 61 yards. What is the total length of the fence?

[_____] _____
                unit

6. A playground game is outlined in chalk. Each of the four sides is 48 inches long and there are four right angles. What is the total length of the outline?

[_____] _____
                unit

7. The sandbox has a wood border. The border has sides that are 32 feet, 45 feet, 29 feet, and 61 feet. What is distance around the sandbox?

[_____] _____
                unit

Add Three and Four Lengths

▶ Distance Around Shapes at Home

Solve.   **Show your work.**

---

8. A border outlines a flowerbed.
How long is the border?

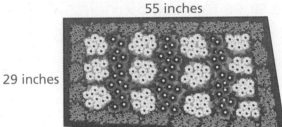

55 inches
29 inches   32 inches
60 inches

☐ _____
unit

---

9. The pantry has a tiled floor.
What is the distance around
the tiled floor?

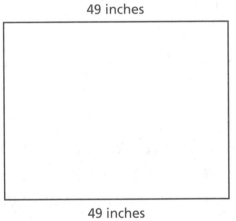

49 inches
24 inches   24 inches
49 inches

☐ _____
unit

---

10. In spring, all of the wood floors
get waxed. This part of the
kitchen was waxed. What is the
distance around the waxed part?

13 feet   12 feet
21 feet

☐ _____
unit

▶ Distance Around Shapes at School

Solve.

Show your work.

11. A picture hanging in the library has sides that are 39 inches, 28 inches, 39 inches, and 28 inches. What is the distance around the picture?

☐ _____
unit

12. The second grade makes an art project. The lengths of the sides of the project are 18 inches, 24 inches, and 19 inches. The teacher wants to frame the project with tape. How much tape does she need?

☐ _____
unit

13. The cafeteria is a square room. Each side measures 47 feet. What is the distance around the room?

☐ _____
unit

14. The school patio has 4 sides. The lengths of the sides are 22 feet, 18 feet, 27 feet, and 16 feet. What is the distance around the patio?

☐ _____
unit

Add Three and Four Lengths

►Solve and Discuss

Solve.   **Show your work.**

1. Jorge is building shelves. The bottom shelf is
   64 inches long. The top shelf is 27 inches longer.
   How long is the top shelf?

   _____

2. The top of a bookcase is 24 inches from the ceiling.
   The ceiling is 96 inches tall. How tall is the bookcase?

   _____

3. Henry is putting a border of rocks around his garden.
   The lengths of the sides of the garden are 12 feet,
   19 feet, and 27 feet. How long will the border be?

   _____

4. Brendan is knitting a scarf. It is 28 centimeters long.
   Then he knits 18 centimeters more. How long is the
   scarf now?

   _____

▶ Length Word Problems

Solve.

Show your work.

5. Hannah has a red ribbon and a blue ribbon. The red ribbon is 17 cm long. The blue ribbon is 13 cm long. How much longer is the red ribbon than the blue ribbon?

_____

6. A roll of tape is 76 feet long to start. Karl uses 24 feet of the tape. How much tape is left?

_____

7. Nick and Ben are running a relay race. Nick runs 48 meters. Ben runs 37 meters. How many fewer meters does Ben run?

_____

8. Candace is putting a fence around her garden. The garden has 4 sides and 4 right angles. Each side of the garden is 23 feet long. How long will the fence be?

_____

More Length Word Problems

▶ Length Word Problems

Solve.   **Show your work.**

9. Caroline uses tape to mark off the space where new grass was planted. The lengths of the sides of the space are 16 feet, 28 feet, 36 feet, and 18 feet. How much tape is needed?

   _____

10. Lauren pulls the shade down. It covers 24 inches of the window. Jessica pulls it down 48 more inches. What is the length of the shade now?

   _____

11. A flagpole is 62 feet tall. The flag covers 11 feet of the pole. How long is the part not covered by the flag?

   _____

12. Miguel is putting a string of lights around a sign. The lengths of the sides of the sign are 26 inches, 18 inches, 26 inches, and 18 inches. What length of lights does he need?

   _____

▶ What's the Error?

I'm trying to add 57 and 29. I'm not sure what to do next.

57 + 29 = ▭

13. Show how to use the number line diagram to find the total.

57 + 29 = ▭

▶ Number Line Diagrams

Represent each equation on the number line diagram.
Then find the difference or the total.

14. 43 + ▭ = 72

15. ▭ + 28 = 86

More Length Word Problems

Name _____

CA CC Content Standards 2.G.3
Mathematical Practices MP.1, MP.3, MP.5, MP.6, MP.8

► Math and Flags

Ships can use flags to send messages.
A flag can be used alone to send a message.
A group of flags can be used to spell out
a message.

This flag means "I have a pilot on board."
It can also be used for the letter H.

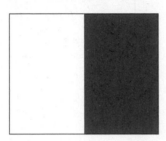

1. How many parts does the flag have?

_____ parts

2. Does the flag show equal parts?

yes   no

This flag means "Return to ship."
It can also be used for the letter P.

3. How many parts does the flag have?

_____ parts

4. Does the flag show equal parts?

yes   no

▶ Square Flags

5. Draw a square flag. Show halves. Color the flag. Color a half of the flag blue.

6. Draw a square flag. Show thirds. Color the flag. Color a third of the flag red.

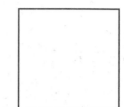

▶ Rectangular Flags

7. Show 4 equal shares that are rectangles.

8. Show 4 equal shares that are triangles.

9. On a separate sheet of paper, design your own flag. Use equal parts. Color your flag.

Focus on Mathematical Practices

1. Write how many in each row and in each column.

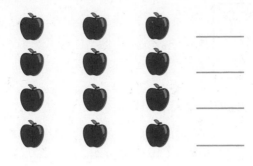

_____

_____

_____

_____

_____ _____ _____

2. Does the equation match the array above?
   Choose Yes or No.

$3 + 3 + 3 = 9$	○ Yes	○ No
$4 + 4 + 4 = 12$	○ Yes	○ No
$3 + 3 + 3 + 3 = 12$	○ Yes	○ No
$4 + 4 + 4 + 4 = 16$	○ Yes	○ No

3. Measure in centimeters.
   Draw rows and columns. Write
   the number of small squares.

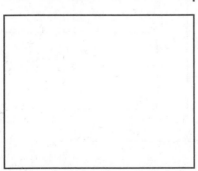

   _____ squares

4. Measure in inches.
   Draw rows and columns. Write
   the number of small squares.

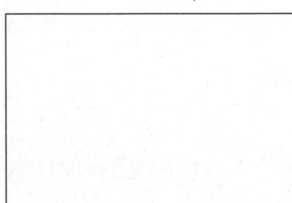

   _____ squares

5. Look at these shapes.

Are the shaded parts the same shape? Explain.

_____

Are the shaded parts the same size? Explain.

_____

_____

6. Draw lines in each shape to make equal shares.

Two Halves	Three Thirds	Four Fourths
◯	◯	◯
▭	▭	▭

7. Choose the squares that show a third shaded.

   ○   ○   ○   ○   ○

    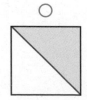

Solve. Circle the number to complete the sentence.

8. Jennifer has 66 inches of red yarn. She has
   14 more inches of blue yarn than red yarn. How
   many inches of blue yarn does Jennifer have?

   Jennifer has $\boxed{\begin{array}{c} 70 \\ 80 \\ 90 \end{array}}$ inches of blue yarn.

9. Elizabeth is shoveling snow from a sidewalk
   that is 20 feet long. So far she has shoveled
   6 feet of the sidewalk. How many more feet
   does she need to shovel?

   Elizabeth needs to shovel $\boxed{\begin{array}{c} 14 \\ 16 \\ 26 \end{array}}$ more feet.

Write an equation and solve.

10. Jake is using fencing to make a dog pen. The pen
    has three sides. Two sides are 6 feet long. The
    third side is 3 feet long. How many feet of fencing
    does Jake need?

    _____ = $\boxed{}$ _____

    unit

11. Devon uses gold ribbon to make a border
    around a square picture. Each side of the
    picture is 14 centimeters long. How many
    centimeters of gold ribbon does Devon need?

    _____ = $\boxed{}$ _____

    unit

12. Write a term from a tile to tell how much is shaded.

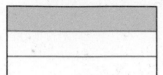

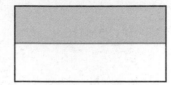

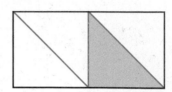

a fourth of   a third of   a half of

_____   _____   _____

13. Complete the equation that the number line diagram represents.

0 5 10 15 20 25 30 35 40 45 50 55 60 65 70 75 80 85 90 95 100

$\boxed{} + 15 = \boxed{}$

14. Represent the equation on the number line diagram.

$46 + 21 =$

0 5 10 15 20 25 30 35 40 45 50 55 60 65 70 75 80 85 90 95 100

Find the total.

$46 + 21 = \boxed{}$

Problem Types

	Result Unknown	Change Unknown	Start Unknown
Add To	Aisha has 46 stamps in her collection. Then her grandfather gives her 29 stamps. How many stamps does she have now? *Situation and Solution Equation[1]:* $46 + 29 = \square$	Aisha has 46 stamps in her collection. Then her grandfather gives her some stamps. Now she has 75 stamps. How many stamps did her grandfather give her? *Situation Equation:* $46 + \square = 75$ *Solution Equation:* $\square = 75 - 46$	Aisha has some stamps in her collection. Then her grandfather gives her 29 stamps. Now she has 75 stamps. How many stamps did she have to start? *Situation Equation:* $\square + 29 = 75$ *Solution Equation:* $\square = 75 - 29$
Take From	A store has 43 bottles of water at the start of the day. During the day, the store sells 25 bottles. How many bottles do they have at the end of the day? *Situation and Solution Equation:* $43 - 25 = \square$	A store has 43 bottles of water at the start of the day. The store has 18 bottles left at the end of the day. How many bottles does the store sell? *Situation Equation:* $43 - \square = 18$ *Solution Equation:* $\square = 43 - 18$	A store sells 25 bottles of water during one day. At the end of the day 18 bottles are left. How many bottles did the store have at the beginning of the day? *Situation Equation:* $\square - 25 = 18$ *Solution Equation:* $\square = 25 + 18$

[1]A situation equation represents the structure (action) in the problem situation. A solution equation shows the operation used to find the answer.

Problem Types continued

Problem Types (continued)

	Total Unknown	Addend Unknown	Both Addends Unknown
Put Together/ Take Apart	A clothing store has 39 shirts with short sleeves and 45 shirts with long sleeves. How many shirts does the store have in all? *Math Drawing²:* 39 45 *Situation and Solution Equation:* $39 + 45 = \square$	Of the 84 shirts in a clothing store, 39 have short sleeves. The rest have long sleeves. How many shirts have long sleeves? *Math Drawing:* 84 39 *Situation Equation:* $84 = 39 + \square$ *Solution Equation:* $84 - 39 = \square$	Pam has 24 roses. How many can she put in her red vase and how many in her blue vase? *Math Drawing:* 24 *Situation Equation:* $24 = \square + \square$

²These math drawings are called Math Mountains in Grades 1–3 and break-apart drawings in Grades 4 and 5.

	Difference Unknown	**Greater Unknown**	**Smaller Unknown**
Compare[1]	Alex has 64 trading cards. Lucy has 48 trading cards. How many **more** trading cards does **Alex** have than Lucy? Lucy has 48 trading cards. Alex has 64 trading cards. How many **fewer** trading cards does **Lucy** have than Alex? *Math Drawing:* A [64] L [48] (?) *Situation Equation:* $48 + \square = 64$ or $\square = 64 - 48$ *Solution Equation:* $\square = 64 - 48$	**Leading Language** Lucy has 48 trading cards. **Alex** has **16 more** trading cards than Lucy. How many trading cards does Alex have? **Misleading Language** Lucy has 48 trading cards. **Lucy** has **16 fewer** trading cards than Alex. How many trading cards does Alex have? *Math Drawing:* A [?] L [48] (16) *Situation and Solution Equation:* $48 + 16 = \square$	**Leading Language** Alex has 64 trading cards. **Lucy** has **16 fewer** trading cards than Alex. How many trading cards does Lucy have? **Misleading Language** Alex has 64 trading cards. **Alex** has **16 more** trading cards than Lucy. How many trading cards does Lucy have? *Math Drawing:* A [64] L [?] (16) *Situation Equation:* $\square + 16 = 64$ or $\square = 64 - 16$ *Solution Equation:* $\square = 64 - 16$

[1]A comparison sentence can always be said in two ways. One way uses *more*, and the other uses *fewer* or *less*. Misleading language suggests the wrong operation. For example, it says *Lucy has 16 fewer trading cards than Alex*, but you have to add 16 cards to the number of cards Lucy has to get the number of cards Alex has.

Glossary

5-groups

|||| |||| tens in 5-groups

○○○○○
○○○○○   ones in 5-groups

A

add

●●●● ●●

$$4 + 2 = 6$$

addend

$$5 + 6 = 11$$

addends

Adding Up Method (for Subtraction)

$$\begin{array}{r} 144 \\ -\ 68 \\ \hline 76 \end{array}$$

$$68 + 2 = 70$$
$$70 + 30 = 100$$
$$100 + 44 = 144$$
$$\boxed{76}$$

addition doubles

Both addends (or partners) are the same.

$$4 + 4 = 8$$

A.M.

Use A.M. for times between midnight and noon.

analog clock

angle

These are angles.

array

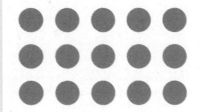

This rectangular array has 3 rows and 5 columns.

bar graph

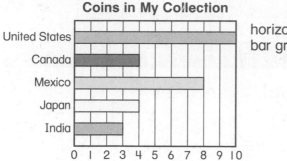

Coins in My Collection

horizontal bar graph

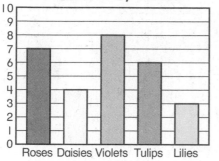

Flowers in My Garden

vertical bar graph

break-apart

You can break apart a larger number to get two smaller amounts called break-aparts.

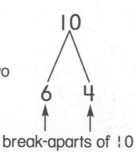

break-aparts of 10

 C

cent

front   back

I cent or I ¢ or $0.01

centimeter (cm)

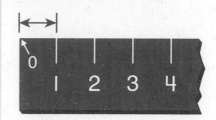

cent sign

56¢

↑

cent sign

clock

analog clock

digital clock

column

This rectangular array has 4 columns with 3 tiles in each column.

compare numbers

Compare numbers using >, <, or =.

$$52 > 25$$
$$25 < 52$$
$$25 = 25$$

comparison bars

Mike	

Sue

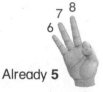

You can add labels and fill in numbers to help you solve *Compare* problems.

count all

$$5 + 3 = \square$$

1 2 3 4 5 6 7 8

● ● ● ● ● | ● ● ●

$$5 + 3 = \boxed{8}$$

count on

$$5 + 3 = \boxed{8}$$

$$5 + \boxed{3} = 8$$

$$8 - 5 = \boxed{3}$$

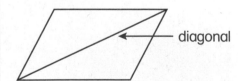

Already **5**

cube

D

data

	Sisters	Brothers
Kendra	2	1
Scott	2	0
Ida	0	1

data

The data in the table show how many sisters and how many brothers each child has.

decade numbers

10, 20, 30, 40, 50, 60, 70, 80, 90

decimal point

$4.25

decimal point

diagonal

diagonal

difference

$$11 - 3 = 8$$

$$
\begin{array}{r}
11 \\
-\ 3 \\
\hline
\text{difference} \longrightarrow \quad 8
\end{array}
$$

digital clock

12:30

digits

0, 1, 2, 3, 4, 5, 6, 7, 8, 9

15 is a 2-digit number.

The 1 in 15 means 1 ten.

The 5 in 15 means 5 ones.

dime

front   back

10 cents or 10¢ or $0.10

dollar

 front

 back

100 cents or

100¢ or $1.00

dollar sign

$4.25
↑
dollar sign

doubles minus 1

$7 + 7 = 14$, so

$7 + 6 = 13$, 1 less than 14.

doubles minus 2

$7 + 7 = 14$, so

$7 + 5 = 12$, 2 less than 14.

doubles plus 1

$6 + 6 = 12$, so

$6 + 7 = 13$, 1 more than 12.

doubles plus 2

$6 + 6 = 12$, so

$6 + 8 = 14$, 2 more than 12.

E

equal shares

2 halves   4 fourths

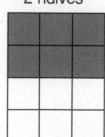   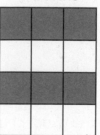

equal to (=)

$$5 + 3 = 8$$

5 plus 3 is equal to 8.

equation

$$4 + 3 = 7 \qquad 7 = 4 + 3$$
$$9 - 5 = 4 \qquad 4 + 5 = 8 + 1$$

An equation must have an = sign.

equation chain

$$3 + 4 = 5 + 2 = 8 - 1 = 7$$

estimate

Make a reasonable guess about how many or how much.

even number

A number is even if you can make groups of 2 and have none left over.

8 is an even number.

exact change

I will pay with 4 dimes and 3 pennies. That is the exact change. I won't get any money back.

expanded form

$$283 = 200 + 80 + 3$$

Expanded Method (for Addition)

$$
\begin{array}{r}
78 = 70 + 8 \\
+\,57 = \underline{50 + 7} \\
120 + 15 = 135
\end{array}
$$

Expanded Method (for Subtraction)

$$
\begin{array}{r}
\overset{50 \quad 14}{64} = \cancel{60} + \cancel{4} \\
-\,28 = \underline{20 + 8} \\
30 + 6 = 36
\end{array}
$$

extra information

Franny has 8 kittens and 2 dogs. 4 kittens are asleep. How many kittens are awake?

$$8 - 4 = \boxed{4}$$

The number of dogs is extra information. It is not needed to solve the problem.

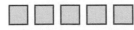

F

fewer

There are fewer ☐ than △.

foot (ft)

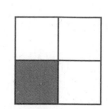

foot

12 inches = 1 foot   (not drawn to scale)

fourth

square

The picture shows 4 fourths. A fourth of the square is shaded.

greater than (>)

34   >   25

34 is greater than 25.

greatest

25   41   63

63 is the greatest number.

group name

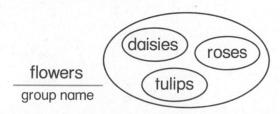

flowers
———
group name

---

half

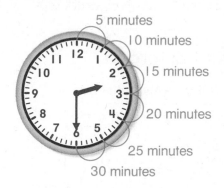

square

The picture shows 2 halves. A half of the square is shaded.

half hour

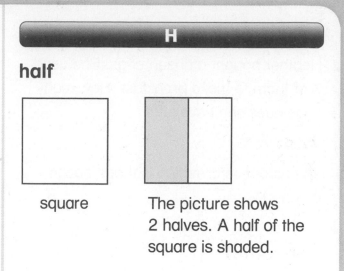

30 minutes = 1 half hour

hexagon

A hexagon has 6 sides and 6 angles.

hidden information

Heather bought a dozen eggs. She used 7 of them to make breakfast. How many eggs does she have left?

$12 - 7 = \boxed{5}$

The hidden information is that a dozen means 12.

horizontal

$4 + 5 = 9$

horizontal form   horizontal line

horizontal bar graph

Coins in My Collection

hour

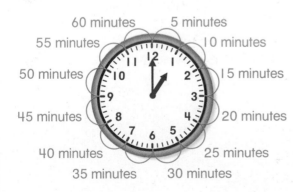

60 minutes = 1 hour

hour hand

hour hand

hundreds

3 hundreds

347 has 3 hundreds.

↑ hundreds

inch (in.)

1 inch

least

14   7   63

7 is the least number.

length

The length of the pencil is about 17 cm.
(not to scale)

less than (<)

$$45 \quad < \quad 46$$

45 is less than 46.

line plot

Length of Shoelaces (inches)

line segment

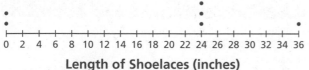

make a ten

$$8 + 6 = \boxed{}$$

8 •• | ••••

10 + 4
10 + 4 = 14,
so 8 + 6 = 14

matching drawing

OOO   fewer
OOOOOOO   more

Math Mountain

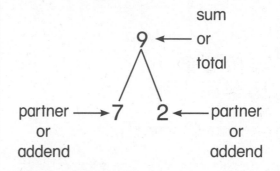

partner   partner
or   or
addend   addend

meter(m)

100 centimeters = 1 meter
(not drawn to scale)

minus

$$8 - 3 = 5$$

$$\begin{array}{r} 8 \\ -\ 3 \\ \hline 5 \end{array}$$

8 minus 3 equals 5.

minute

60 seconds = 1 minute

minute hand

minute hand: points to the minutes

more

There are more ◯ than ▢.

N

New Groups Above Method

$$
\begin{array}{r}
\overset{1}{5}6 \\
+\ 28 \\
\hline
84
\end{array}
$$

$6 + 8 = 14$

The 1 new ten in 14 goes up to the tens place.

New Groups Below Method

$$
\begin{array}{r}
56 \\
+\ 28 \\
\overset{1}{} \\
\hline
84
\end{array}
$$

$6 + 8 = 14$

The 1 new ten in 14 goes below in the tens place.

nickel

front   back

5 cents or 5¢ or $0.05

not equal to (≠)

$6 + 4 \neq 8$

$6 + 4$ is not equal to 8.

number line diagram

This is a number line diagram.

number name

12

twelve ⟵ number name

O

odd number

A number is odd if you can make groups of 2 and have one left over.

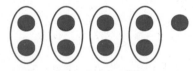

9 is an odd number.

ones

7 ones

347 has 7 ones.

↑
ones

opposite operations

Addition and subtraction are opposite operations.

$$5 + 9 = 14$$
$$14 - 9 = 5$$

Use addition to check subtraction. Use subtraction to check addition.

opposite sides

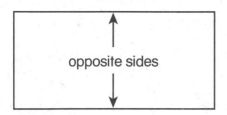

opposite sides

order

2, 5, 6

The numbers 2, 5, and 6 are in order from least to greatest.

P

pair

A group of 2 is a pair.

The picture shows 4 pairs of counters.

partner lengths

partner lengths of 4 cm

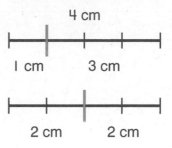

4 cm

1 cm   3 cm

2 cm   2 cm

partners

$$9 + 6 = 15$$

partners (addends)

penny

front   back

1 cent or 1¢ or $0.01

pentagon

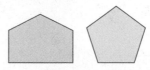

A pentagon has 5 sides and 5 angles.

picture graph

Flowers	🌼 🌼 🌼 🌼 🌼 🌼 🌼
Vases	🏺 🏺 🏺 🏺 🏺 🏺 🏺 🏺 🏺

plus

$$3 + 2 = 5$$

3 plus 2 equals 5.

$$\begin{array}{r} 3 \\ + 2 \\ \hline 5 \end{array}$$

P.M.

Use P.M. for times between noon and midnight.

proof drawing

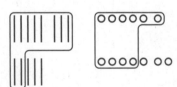

$$86 + 57 = 143$$

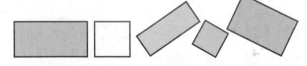

Q

quadrilateral

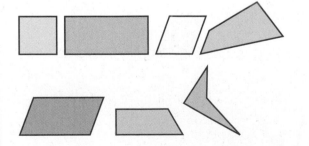

A quadrilateral has 4 sides and 4 angles.

quarter

front   back

25 cents or 25¢ or $0.25

A quarter is another name for a fourth.

A quarter is a fourth of a dollar.

quick hundreds

347

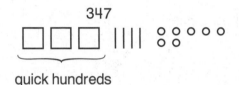

quick hundreds

quick tens

162

quick tens

R

rectangle

A rectangle has 4 sides and 4 right angles. Opposite sides have the same length.

rectangular prism

right angle

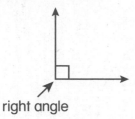

right angle

A right angle is sometimes called a *square corner*.

round

Express a number to the nearest ten or hundred. You can round down or round up.

$$52 \longrightarrow 50 \qquad 278 \longrightarrow 300$$

row

This rectangular array has 3 rows with 4 tiles in each row.

ruler

A ruler is used to measure length.

scale

Coins in My Collection

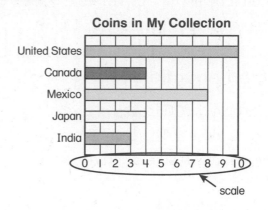

scale

The numbers along the side or the bottom of a graph.

Show All Totals Method

$$
\begin{array}{r}
25 \\
+\ 48 \\
\hline
60 \\
13 \\
\hline
73
\end{array}
\qquad
\begin{array}{r}
724 \\
+\ 158 \\
\hline
800 \\
70 \\
12 \\
\hline
882
\end{array}
$$

situation equation

A baker baked 100 loaves of bread. He sold some loaves. There are 73 loaves left. How many loaves of bread did he sell?

$$100 - \boxed{} = 73$$

situation equation

© Houghton Mifflin Harcourt Publishing Company

skip count

skip count by 2s: 2, 4, 6, 8, . . .
skip count by 5s: 5, 10, 15, 20, . . .
skip count by 10s: 10, 20, 30, 40, 50, . . .

solution equation

A baker baked 100 loaves of bread. He sold some loaves. There are 73 loaves left. How many loaves of bread did he sell?

$$100 - 73 = \boxed{}$$

solution equation

square

A square has 4 equal sides and 4 right angles.

subtract

$$8 - 5 = 3$$

subtraction doubles

Both addends or partners are the same.

$$8 - 4 = 4$$

sum

$$4 + 3 = 7$$

$$\begin{array}{r} 4 \\ +\ 3 \\ \hline 7 \end{array}$$

sum ⟶

survey

When you collect data by asking people questions, you are taking a survey.

teen number

any number from 11 to 19

11 12 13 14 15 16 17 18 19

tens

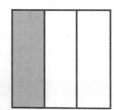

4 tens

347 has 4 tens.
↑
tens

third

square

The picture shows 3 thirds. A third of the square is shaded.

thousand

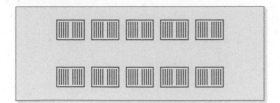

1,000 = ten hundreds

total

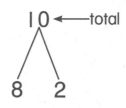

10 ←—— total

8   2

triangle

A triangle has 3 sides and 3 angles.

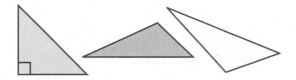
U

ungroup

Ungroup when you need more ones or tens to subtract.

Ungroup First Method

$$64$$
$$-28$$
↑   ↑
yes no

1. Check to see if there are enough tens and ones to subtract.

5 14
6̸ 1̸4̸
$$-28$$

2. You can get more ones by taking from the tens and putting them in the ones place.

5 14
6̸ 1̸4̸
$$-28$$
$$36$$

3. Subtract from either right to left or left to right.

unknown addend

$$3 + \boxed{} = 9$$

↑
unknown addend

unknown total

$$3 + 6 = \boxed{}$$

↑
unknown total

V

vertical

$$4$$
$$+3$$
$$7$$

vertical form   vertical line

vertical bar graph

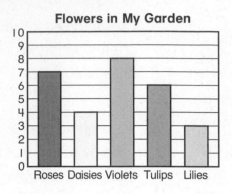

Flowers in My Garden

view

This is the side view of the rectangular prism above.

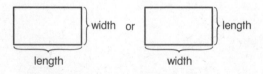

W

width

width or length

length width

Y

yard (yd)

3 feet = 1 yard (not drawn to scale)

California Common Core Standards for Mathematical Content

2.OA Operations and Algebraic Thinking

Represent and solve problems involving addition and subtraction.

2.OA.1	Use addition and subtraction within 100 to solve one- and two-step word problems involving situations of adding to, taking from, putting together, taking apart, and comparing, with unknowns in all positions, e.g., by using drawings and equations with a symbol for the unknown number to represent the problem.	Unit 1 Lessons 1, 2, 4, 10, 11, 12, 13, 14, 15, 16, 17, 18, 19, 20, 21; Unit 2 Lessons 1, 2, 7, 15; Unit 4 Lessons 3, 4, 5, 12, 13, 14, 16, 17, 18, 19, 20, 21, 22, 23; Unit 5 Lessons 3, 4, 5, 6, 7, 9, 10; Unit 6 Lessons 8, 9, 14, 15; Unit 7 Lessons 3, 4, 5 **Daily Routine:** Money Routine

Add and subtract within 20.

2.OA.2	Fluently add and subtract within 20 using mental strategies. By end of Grade 2, know from memory all sums of two one-digit numbers.	Unit 1 Lessons 1, 2, 3, 4, 5, 7, 8, 9, 10, 11, 12, 13, 14, 15, 16, 17, 18, 19, 20, 21; Unit 2 Lessons 1, 2, 6; Unit 3 Lessons 1, 2, 3, 4; Unit 4 Lessons 6, 13; Unit 5 Lessons 3, 4, 5, 9, 10 **Quick Practices:** Unknown Addend; Stay or Go?; Equation Chains; Blue Math Mountain Cards; Dive the Deep; Make-a-Ten Cards: Addition; Make-a-Ten Cards: Subtraction; Addition Sprint; Subtraction Sprint; Teen Addition Flash; Teen Subtraction Flash

Work with equal groups of objects to gain foundations for multiplication.

2.OA.3	Determine whether a group of objects (up to 20) has an odd or even number of members, e.g., by pairing objects or counting them by 2s; write an equation to express an even number as a sum of two equal addends.	Unit 1 Lessons 6, 7, 21; Unit 7 Lesson 1 **Quick Practices:** Count by 2s, Even or Odd?
2.OA.4	Use addition to find the total number of objects arranged in rectangular arrays with up to 5 rows and up to 5 columns; write an equation to express the total as a sum of equal addends.	Unit 7 Lessons 1, 6

2.NBT Number and Operations in Base Ten

Understand place value.

2.NBT.1	Understand that the three digits of a three-digit number represent amounts of hundreds, tens, and ones; e.g., 706 equals 7 hundreds, 0 tens, and 6 ones.	Unit 2 Lessons 1, 2, 3, 4, 5, 6, 7, 8, 9, 10, 11; Unit 4 Lessons 7, 8, 9, 10, 12 ,14; Unit 6 Lesson 2 **Daily Routines:** Comparing 2-Digit Numbers, Comparing 3-Digit Numbers **Quick Practices:** Tens Talking; Unscramble the Hundreds, Tens, and Ones

2.NBT.1a	Understand that the three digits of a three-digit number represent amounts of hundreds, tens, and ones; e.g., 706 equals 7 hundreds, 0 tens, and 6 ones. Understand the following as special cases: **a.** 100 can be thought of as a bundle of ten tens—called a "hundred."	Unit 2 Lessons 1, 2, 3, 4, 6, 7, 8, 9, 11; Unit 4 Lessons 3, 4, 7, 8, 9, 10, 12, 14; Unit 6 Lessons 1, 4 **Quick Practice:** Tens Talking
2.NBT.1b	Understand that the three digits of a three-digit number represent amounts of hundreds, tens, and ones; e.g., 706 equals 7 hundreds, 0 tens, and 6 ones. Understand the following as special cases: **b.** The numbers 100, 200, 300, 400, 500, 600, 700, 800, 900 refer to one, two, three, four, five, six, seven, eight, or nine hundreds (and 0 tens and 0 ones).	Unit 4 Lesson 7; Unit 6 Lessons 1, 4
2.NBT.2	Count within 1000; skip-count by 2s, 5s, 10s, and 100s.	Unit 1 Lesson 6; Unit 2 Lessons 1, 2, 3, 12, 15; Unit 4 Lesson 15; Unit 5 Lesson 2; Unit 6 Lessons 1, 4 **Daily Routines:** Money Routine; Comparing 2-Digit Numbers; Dimes, Nickels, Pennies **Quick Practices:** Count by 2s, Count by 10s to 120, Count by 10s from 130 to 240, Count by 1s from 1 to 50, Count by 1s from 51 to 100, Count by 1s from 100 to 150, Count by 1s from 150 to 200, Count by 5s from 5 to 100, Count by 5s from 100 to 200, Count by 10s to 200, Count by 100s to 1,000
2.NBT.3	Read and write numbers to 1000 using base-ten numerals, number names, and expanded form.	Unit 2 Lessons 1, 2, 3, 4, 5; Unit 6 Lessons 1, 2, 4 **Daily Routines:** Money Routine, Comparing 2-Digit Numbers, Comparing 3-Digit Numbers **Quick Practices:** Teen Machine; Unscramble the Hundreds, Tens, and Ones
2.NBT.4	Compare two three-digit numbers based on meanings of the hundreds, tens, and ones digits, using >, =, and < symbols to record the results of comparisons.	Unit 2 Lessons 5, 15; Unit 3 Lesson 6; Unit 5 Lesson 10; Unit 6 Lessons 3, 15 **Daily Routines:** Comparing 2-Digit Numbers, Comparing 3-Digit Numbers

Use place value understanding and properties of operations to add and subtract.

2.NBT.5	Fluently add and subtract within 100 using strategies based on place value, properties of operations, and/or the relationship between addition and subtraction.	Unit 1 Lessons 9, 16; Unit 2 Lessons 2, 4, 13, 14, 15; Unit 3 Lesson 9; Unit 4 Lessons 3, 4, 5, 6, 11, 12, 13, 14, 15, 17, 18, 19, 20, 21, 22, 23; Unit 5 Lessons 5, 7, 8; Unit 6 Lessons 3, 8, 10, 15; Unit 7 Lessons 4, 5 **Daily Routines:** Money Routine, Math Mountains for 100 or 2-Digit **Quick Practice:** Quick check

2.NBT.6	Add up to four two-digit numbers using strategies based on place value and properties of operations.	Unit 1 Lesson 9; Unit 2 Lessons 6, 8, 9, 10, 14; Unit 4 Lessons 14, 15; Unit 7 Lessons 4, 5
2.NBT.7	Add and subtract within 1000, using concrete models or drawings and strategies based on place value, properties of operations, and/or the relationship between addition and subtraction; relate the strategy to a written method. Understand that in adding or subtracting three-digit numbers, one adds or subtracts hundreds and hundreds, tens and tens, ones and ones; and sometimes it is necessary to compose or decompose tens or hundreds.	Unit 2 Lessons 4, 6, 7, 8, 9, 10, 11, 14, 15; Unit 4 Lessons 1, 2, 3, 5, 6, 7, 8, 9, 10, 12, 13, 15, 16, 17, 23; Unit 6 Lessons 2, 5, 6, 7, 8, 9, 10, 11, 12, 13, 14, 15 **Daily Routine:** Money Routine **Quick Practice:** Add Over the Hundred
2.NBT.7.1	Use estimation strategies to make reasonable estimates in problem solving.	Unit 4 Lesson 14; Unit 6 Lesson 12
2.NBT.8	Mentally add 10 or 100 to a given number 100–900, and mentally subtract 10 or 100 from a given number 100–900.	Unit 2 Lesson 4; Unit 6 Lessons 2, 4 **Quick Practices:** Trios, Add or Subtract 100, Add or Subtract 10
2.NBT. 9	Explain why addition and subtraction strategies work, using place value and the properties of operations.	Unit 1 Lessons 1, 3, 9; Unit 2 Lessons 2, 4, 6, 7, 8, 9, 10; Unit 4 Lessons 3, 4, 5, 6, 7, 8, 9, 10, 12, 14, 15, 16, 17, 18; Unit 6 Lessons 2, 5, 6, 7, 8, 9, 10, 11, 12, 13, 15 **Daily Routine:** Money Routine **Quick Practice:** Make-a-Ten Cards: Addition; Make-a-Ten Cards: Subtraction

2.MD Measurement and Data

Measure and estimate lengths in standard units.

2.MD.1	Measure the length of an object by selecting and using appropriate tools such as rulers, yardsticks, meter sticks, and measuring tapes.	Unit 3 Lessons 1, 2, 3, 4, 6, 7, 8, 9; Unit 4 Lesson 23; Unit 7 Lesson 1
2.MD.2	Measure the length of an object twice, using length units of different lengths for the two measurements; describe how the two measurements relate to the size of the unit chosen.	Unit 3 Lessons 7, 8, 9
2.MD.3	Estimate lengths using units of inches, feet, centimeters, and meters.	Unit 3 Lessons 3, 4, 6, 7, 8; Unit 4 Lesson 23 **Daily Routine:** Estimating Units of Length
2.MD.4	Measure to determine how much longer one object is than another, expressing the length difference in terms of a standard length unit.	Unit 3 Lessons 1, 2, 6; Unit 4 Lesson 23

Relate addition and subtraction to length.

2.MD.5	Use addition and subtraction within 100 to solve word problems involving lengths that are given in the same units, e.g., by using drawings (such as drawings of rulers) and equations with a symbol for the unknown number to represent the problem.	Unit 4 Lesson 23; Unit 7 Lessons 3, 4, 5

2.MD.6	Represent whole numbers as lengths from 0 on a number line diagram with equally spaced points corresponding to the numbers 0, 1, 2, . . ., and represent whole-number sums and differences within 100 on a number line diagram.	Unit 7 Lessons 3, 5 **Daily Routine:** Comparing 2-Digit Numbers

Work with time and money.

2.MD.7	Tell and write time from analog and digital clocks to the nearest five minutes, using a.m. and p.m. Know relationships of time (e.g., minutes in an hour, days in a month, weeks in a year).	Unit 5 Lessons 1, 2 **Daily Routine:** Time
2.MD.8	Solve word problems involving combinations of dollar bills, quarters, dimes, nickels, and pennies, using $ and ¢ symbols appropriately. Example: *If you have 2 dimes and 3 pennies, how many cents do you have?*	Unit 2 Lessons 11, 12, 15; Unit 4 Lessons 1, 2, 10, 15; Unit 6 Lesson 1 **Daily Routines:** Money Routine; Dimes, Nickels, Pennies; Math Mountains for 100 or 2-Digit Numbers

Represent and interpret data.

2.MD.9	Generate measurement data by measuring lengths of several objects to the nearest whole unit, or by making repeated measurements of the same object. Show the measurements by making a line plot, where the horizontal scale is marked off in whole-number units.	Unit 3 Lessons 6, 7, 8
2.MD.10	Draw a picture graph and a bar graph (with single-unit scale) to represent a data set with up to four categories. Solve simple put-together, take-apart, and compare problems using information presented in a bar graph.	Unit 5 Lessons 3, 4, 5, 6, 7, 8, 9, 10

2.G Geometry

Reason with shapes and their attributes.

2.G.1	Recognize and draw shapes having specified attributes, such as a given number of angles or a given number of equal faces. Identify triangles, quadrilaterals, pentagons, hexagons, and cubes.	Unit 3 Lessons 2, 3, 4, 5, 9; Unit 7 Lessons 1, 2, 4
2.G.2	Partition a rectangle into rows and columns of same-size squares and count to find the total number of them.	Unit 7 Lessons 1, 6
2.G.3	Partition circles and rectangles into two, three, or four equal shares, describe the shares using the words halves, thirds, half of, a third of, etc., and describe the whole as two halves, three thirds, four fourths. Recognize that equal shares of identical wholes need not have the same shape.	Unit 5 Lesson 2; Unit 7 Lessons 1, 2, 6

California Common Core Standards for Mathematical Practice

MP.1 Make sense of problems and persevere in solving them.

Mathematically proficient students start by explaining to themselves the meaning of a problem and looking for entry points to its solution. They analyze givens, constraints, relationships, and goals. They make conjectures about the form and meaning of the solution and plan a solution pathway rather than simply jumping into a solution attempt. They consider analogous problems, and try special cases and simpler forms of the original problem in order to gain insight into its solution. They monitor and evaluate their progress and change course if necessary. Older students might, depending on the context of the problem, transform algebraic expressions or change the viewing window on their graphing calculator to get the information they need. Mathematically proficient students can explain correspondences between equations, verbal descriptions, tables, and graphs or draw diagrams of important features and relationships, graph data, and search for regularity or trends. Younger students might rely on using concrete objects or pictures to help conceptualize and solve a problem. Mathematically proficient students check their answers to problems using a different method, and they continually ask themselves, "Does this make sense?" They can understand the approaches of others to solving complex problems and identify correspondences between different approaches.

Unit 1 Lessons 2, 4, 6, 7, 9, 10, 11, 12, 13, 14, 15, 16, 17, 18, 19, 20, 21

Unit 2 Lessons 1, 2, 3, 4, 5, 6, 7, 8, 9, 11, 12, 13, 14, 15

Unit 3 Lessons 1, 3, 6, 9

Unit 4 Lessons 1, 2, 3, 4, 5, 6, 7, 8, 9, 10, 11, 12, 13, 14, 16, 17, 18, 19, 20, 21, 22, 23

Unit 5 Lessons 1, 3, 4, 5, 6, 7, 8, 9, 10

Unit 6 Lessons 1, 4, 5, 8, 9, 10, 11, 12, 14, 15

Unit 7 Lessons 1, 2, 3, 4, 5, 6

MP.2 Reason abstractly and quantitatively.

Mathematically proficient students make sense of quantities and their relationships in problem situations. They bring two complementary abilities to bear on problems involving quantitative relationships: the ability to *decontextualize*—to abstract a given situation and represent it symbolically and manipulate the representing symbols as if they have a life of their own, without necessarily attending to their referents—and the ability to *contextualize*, to pause as needed during the manipulation process in order to probe into the referents for the symbols involved. Quantitative reasoning entails habits of creating a coherent representation of the problem at hand considering the units involved attending to the meaning of quantities, not just how to compute them and knowing and flexibly using different properties of operations and objects.

Unit 1 Lessons 1, 5, 7, 8, 9, 10, 11, 14, 21

Unit 2 Lessons 1, 3, 4, 5, 6, 7, 8, 9, 11, 12, 13, 14, 15

Unit 3 Lessons 1, 2, 3, 7, 8, 9

Unit 4 Lessons 1, 2, 3, 4, 5, 6, 7, 8, 9, 10, 11, 12, 13, 14, 15, 17, 19, 20, 22, 23

Unit 5 Lessons 1, 2, 5,10

Unit 6 Lessons 1, 2, 4, 10, 12, 15

Unit 7 Lessons 1, 2, 3, 4, 5, 6

MP.3 Construct viable arguments and critique the reasoning of others.

Mathematically proficient students understand and use stated assumptions, definitions, and previously established results in constructing arguments. They make conjectures and build a logical progression of statements to explore the truth of their conjectures. They are able to analyze situations by breaking them into cases, and can recognize and use counterexamples. They justify their conclusions, communicate them to others, and respond to the arguments of others. They reason inductively about data, making plausible arguments that take into account the context from which the data arose. Mathematically proficient students are also able to compare the effectiveness of two plausible arguments, distinguish correct logic or reasoning from that which is flawed, and—if there is a flaw in an argument—explain what it is. Elementary students can construct arguments using concrete referents such as objects, drawings, diagrams, and actions. Such arguments can make sense and be correct, even though they are not generalized or made formal until later grades. Later, students learn to determine domains to which an argument applies. Students at all grades can listen or read the arguments of others, decide whether they make sense, and ask useful questions to clarify or improve the arguments.

Unit 1 Lessons 1, 3, 4, 6, 7, 8, 9, 10, 11, 12, 13, 14, 15, 16, 17, 18, 19, 20, 21

Unit 2 Lessons 2, 3, 4, 5, 6, 7, 8, 9, 10, 12, 13, 14, 15

Unit 3 Lessons 1, 2, 3, 4, 5, 6, 7, 8, 9

Unit 4 Lessons 1, 2, 3, 4, 5, 6, 7, 8, 9, 10, 11, 12, 13, 14, 15, 16, 17, 18, 19, 20, 21, 22, 23

Unit 5 Lessons 1, 2, 3, 4, 5, 6, 7, 8, 9, 10

Unit 6 Lessons 1, 2, 3, 4, 5, 6, 7, 8, 9, 10, 11, 12, 13, 14, 15

Unit 7 Lessons 1, 2, 3, 4, 5, 6

MP.4 Model with mathematics.

Mathematically proficient students can apply the mathematics they know to solve problems arising in everyday life, society, and the workplace. In early grades, this might be as simple as writing an addition equation to describe a situation. In middle grades, a student might apply proportional reasoning to plan a school event or analyze a problem in the community. By high school, a student might use geometry to solve a design problem or use a function to describe how one quantity of interest depends on another. Mathematically proficient students who can apply what they know are comfortable making assumptions and approximations to simplify a complicated situation, realizing that these may need revision later. They are able to identify important quantities in a practical situation and map their relationships using such tools as diagrams, two-way tables, graphs, flowcharts and formulas. They can analyze those relationships mathematically to draw conclusions. They routinely interpret their mathematical results in the context of the situation and reflect on whether the results make sense, possibly improving the model if it has not served its purpose.

Unit 1 Lessons 10, 11, 12, 13, 15, 16, 17, 18, 19, 20, 21

Unit 2 Lessons 4, 6, 7, 11, 12, 14, 15

Unit 3 Lessons 6, 7, 8, 9

Unit 4 Lessons 3, 4, 5, 7, 10, 12, 13, 18, 19, 20, 21, 23

Unit 5 Lessons 3, 5, 8, 9, 10

Unit 6 Lessons 9, 11, 14, 15

Unit 7 Lessons 3, 6

MP.5 Use appropriate tools strategically.

Mathematically proficient students consider the available tools when solving a mathematical problem. These tools might include pencil and paper, concrete models, a ruler, a protractor, a calculator, a spreadsheet, a computer algebra system, a statistical package, or dynamic geometry software. Proficient students are sufficiently familiar with tools appropriate for their grade or course to make sound decisions about when each of these tools might be helpful, recognizing both the insight to be gained and their limitations. For example, mathematically proficient high school students analyze graphs of functions and solutions generated using a graphing calculator. They detect possible errors by strategically using estimation and other mathematical knowledge. When making mathematical models, they know that technology can enable them to visualize the results of varying assumptions, explore consequences, and compare predictions with data. Mathematically proficient students at various grade levels are able to identify relevant external mathematical resources, such as digital content located on a website, and use them to pose or solve problems. They are able to use technological tools to explore and deepen their understanding of concepts.

Unit 1 Lessons 3, 4, 6, 20, 21

Unit 2 Lessons 1, 2, 3, 4, 5, 8, 12, 13, 14, 15

Unit 3 Lessons 1, 2, 3, 5, 6, 7, 8, 9

Unit 4 Lessons 1, 2, 3, 4, 7, 8, 9, 11, 15, 18, 23

Unit 5 Lessons 1, 2, 5, 10

Unit 6 Lessons 1, 2, 5, 7, 10, 15

Unit 7 Lessons 1, 2, 3, 6

MP.6 Attend to precision.

Mathematically proficient students try to communicate precisely to others. They try to use clear definitions in discussion with others and in their own reasoning. They state the meaning of the symbols they choose, including using the equal sign consistently and appropriately. They are careful about specifying units of measure, and labeling axes to clarify the correspondence with quantities in a problem. They calculate accurately and efficiently, express numerical answers with a degree of precision appropriate for the problem context. In the elementary grades, students give carefully formulated explanations to each other. By the time they reach high school they have learned to examine claims and make explicit use of definitions.

Unit 1 Lessons 1, 2, 3, 4, 5, 6, 7, 8, 9, 10, 11, 12, 13, 14, 15, 16, 17, 18, 19, 20, 21

Unit 2 Lessons 1, 2, 3, 4, 5, 6, 7, 8, 9, 10, 11, 12, 13, 14, 15

Unit 3 Lessons 1, 2, 3, 4, 5, 6, 7, 8, 9

Unit 4 Lessons 1, 2, 3, 4, 5, 6, 7, 8, 9, 10, 11, 12, 13, 14, 15, 16, 17, 18, 19, 20, 21, 22, 23

Unit 5 Lessons 1, 2, 3, 4, 5, 6, 7, 8, 9, 10

Unit 6 Lessons 1, 2, 3, 4, 5, 6, 7, 8, 9, 10, 11, 12, 13, 14, 15

Unit 7 Lessons 1, 2, 3, 4, 5, 6

MP.7 Look for and make use of structure.

Mathematically proficient students look closely to discern a pattern or structure. Young students, for example, might notice that three and seven more is the same amount as seven and three more, or they may sort a collection of shapes according to how many sides the shapes have. Later, students will see 7×8 equals the well remembered $7 \times 5 + 7 \times 3$, in preparation for learning about the distributive property. In the expression $x^2 + 9x + 14$, older students can see the 14 as 2×7 and the 9 as $2 + 7$. They recognize the significance of an existing line in a geometric figure and can use the strategy of drawing an auxiliary line for solving problems. They also can step back for an overview and shift perspective. They can see complicated things, such as some algebraic expressions, as single objects or as being composed of several objects. For example, they can see $5 - 3(x - y)^2$ as 5 minus a positive number times a square and use that to realize that its value cannot be more than 5 for any real numbers x and y.

Unit 1 Lessons 1, 2, 5, 6, 9, 13, 17, 18, 19, 21

Unit 2 Lessons 1, 2, 3, 4, 6, 10, 11, 12, 15

Unit 3 Lessons 1, 3, 4, 5, 6, 7, 8, 9

Unit 4 Lessons 1, 2, 7, 13, 17, 19, 21, 23

Unit 5 Lessons 2, 6, 7, 10

Unit 6 Lessons 4, 12, 13, 15

Unit 7 Lessons 2, 6

MP.8 Look for and express regularity in repeated reasoning.

Mathematically proficient students notice if calculations are repeated, and look both for general methods and for shortcuts. Upper elementary students might notice when dividing 25 by 11 that they are repeating the same calculations over and over again, and conclude they have a repeating decimal. By paying attention to the calculation of slope as they repeatedly check whether points are on the line through (1, 2) with slope 3, middle school students might abstract the equation $(y - 2)/(x - 1) = 3$. Noticing the regularity in the way terms cancel when expanding $(x - 1)(x + 1)$, $(x - 1)$ $(x^2 + x + 1)$, and $(x - 1)(x^3 + x^2 + x + 1)$ might lead them to the general formula for the sum of a geometric series. As they work to solve a problem, mathematically proficient students maintain oversight of the process, while attending to the details. They continually evaluate the reasonableness of their intermediate results.

Unit 1 Lessons 2, 6, 7, 21

Unit 2 Lessons 5, 10, 11, 15

Unit 3 Lessons 1, 2, 7, 8, 9

Unit 4 Lessons 4, 8, 13, 23

Unit 5 Lessons 2, 10

Unit 6 Lessons 2, 4, 7, 8, 12, 15

Unit 7 Lessons 1, 2, 6

Index

Compare Word Problems. *See* Problem Types.

Comparison. *See also* Problem Types; Symbols.

  language

    fewer, 39–40, 41–42, 53–54, 192, 237, 252

    more, 39–40, 41–42, 53–54, 192, 237, 252

Comparison bars, 39–40, 41–44, 53–54, 59, 205–206, 252, 293–296

Content Overview

  Unit 1, 1–2, 7–8, 29–30

  Unit 2, 71–72, 85–86

  Unit 3, 115–116, 133–134

  Unit 4, 159–160, 171–172

  Unit 5, 221–222, 235–236

  Unit 6, 259–260, 273–274, 283–284

  Unit 7, 303–304

Counting

  by 2s, 17–18

  by 5s, 99–102, 110, 229

  by 10s, 73, 79, 102, 269

  by 100s, 261, 265

  money, 97, 100–102

  over the hundreds, 269

Count On Strategy. *See* Addition: strategies; Subtraction: strategies.

Cubes, 129, 131

Customary Units of Measurement. *See* Measurement.

D

Data. *See also* Bar Graphs, Picture Graphs, Word Problems.

  collect, 138, 144, 147, 150, 239, 247, 254

  organize, 246

  represent, 139–140, 148, 149–151, 249, 253

  tables, 125–126, 127–128, 138, 144, 246–247, 249

Decimal notation, 184

Dime. *See* Coins.

Dollar

  place value representation, 184

  value of, 97–98

Dollar bills, 95–96

Dollar equivalents, 165–166

Dollar sign. *See* Symbols.

Dollars with Penny Array, 261–262

Dot plots, 139–140, 148–151

Drawing

  comparison bars, 39–40, 41–44, 53–54, 59, 205–206, 210, 252, 293–296

  Math Mountains, 6, 24

  money amounts, 102, 167

  numbers, 80, 83–84, 195, 265

  proof drawings, 89, 91–94, 176, 276, 278, 285

  rectangular prisms, 131

© Houghton Mifflin Harcourt Publishing Company

Index (continued)

for addition, 31–32, 33–34, 35–37, 41–42, 43–44, 276, 278

for subtraction, 169, 173–174, 177, 285, 293–296

E

Equal shares

fourths, 309–310, 313–314, 328

halves, 309–310, 313–314

thirds, 309–310, 313–314

Equal sign. *See* Symbols.

Equations. *See also* Addition; Algebra; Problem Types; Subtraction.

chains, 23

relate to Math Mountains, 3, 5–6, 191, 292, 293–296

situation and solution, S1–S3

unknown addend or partner, 15–16, 24, 199–204, 281–282, 294, 326 (*See also* Problem Types)

unknown total, 16, 24, 33–36, 60, 82, 189–190, 205, 207–209, 292, 326 *See also* Problem Types.

vertical form, 24

Estimation

addition and subtraction, 196, 290

length, 125–128, 137–138, 144, 147

Even. *See* Numbers.

Expanded form, 79, 266

Expanded Method

in subtraction *See* Algorithms; Subtraction.

F

Family Letter, 1–2, 7–8, 29–30, 71–72, 85–86, 115–116, 133–134, 159–160, 171–172, 221–222, 235–236, 259–260, 273–274, 283–284, 303–304

Fluency activities and games

New Ten Challenge, 105–106

Ungroup Challenge, 187–188

Fluency practice

addition within 20, 28, 40, 58, 88, 176

addition within 100, 103–106, 193, 202, 210, 240, 248, 268, 282, 288

subtraction within 20, 28, 40, 58, 88, 176

subtraction within 100, 185–188, 193, 202, 210, 282, 288

Fourths, 309–310, 313–314

Fractions

Equal shares, 309–310, 313–314, 328

Time (half-hour), 230

G

Geometry. *See also* Measurement.

angles, 121–124

right, 121–122, 125–126

attributes

corners (angles), 121

faces, 129, 131

sides, 121–124

value of, 97–98, 100–102,
167–168

count the value of coins and bills,
97–98

decimal notation, 184

dollars
place value, 184
value of, 97–98

place value, 184

symbols
cent sign, 97, 184
decimal notation, 184
dollar sign, 97, 184

word problems, 97, 197–198, 213

**Multiplication readiness,
skip-counting**

by 2s, 17–18

by 5s, 99–102, 110, 229

by 10s, 73, 79, 102, 269

by 100s, 261, 265

arrays, 307–308

N

New Groups Below Method, 91, 276

New Ten Challenge, 105–106

Nickel. *See* Coins; Money.

Number-Bond diagram. *See* Math
Mountains.

Number line diagram

addition, 318, 326

subtraction, 318, 326

Number names, 80, 270

Number Path, 80

Numbers. *See also* Counting.

11 through 20, 21–22

21 through 100, 80

101 to 1,000, 73, 77–79, 265–266

compare, 83–84, 267–268

decade numbers, 81

doubles, 20–22

even, 19–20

expanded form, 79, 266

fractions (even shares)
fourths, 309–310, 313–314
halves, 230, 309–310
thirds, 309–310, 313

number names, 80, 270

odd, 19–20

word names for, 80, 270

writing, 73, 80, 270

O

Odd. *See* Numbers.

P

Partners. *See also* Addend.

decade partners of 178, 81

unknown partner, 15–16, 25,
201–202, 281

Path to Fluency

Add and subtract within 20, 28, 40,
58, 88, 176

Index (continued)

Q

R

S

is greater than (>), 83–84, 267–268

is less than (<), 83–84, 267–268

right angle, 121

unknown (□), 24

T

Take From Word Problems. *See* Problem Types.

Tape diagrams. *See* Comparison bars.

Three-dimensional figures. *See* Geometry.

Time

a.m./p.m., 224, 232

analog/digital clock, 223–225, 227–228

calendar, 233–234

half-hour, 230

hour hand, 223, 228

minute hand, 223, 228, 230–231

minutes in an hour, 229, 233

to five minutes, 230–234

to the hour, 227–228

unit relationships, 233

Triangle, 123, 127–128, 132

Two-dimensional figure. *See* Geometry.

Two-step problems. *See* Problem Types.

U

Ungroup 100, 169

Ungroup Challenge, 187–188

Ungroup First Method. *See* Algorithms; Subtraction.

Ungrouping. *See* Algorithms; Subtraction.

Unit Review and Test, 67–70, 111–114, 155–158, 217–220, 255–258, 299–302, 329–332

Unknown addends or partners, 15–16, 38, 44

addition, 199–200, 203–204, 207

count on, 169

Math Mountains, 159–160

subtraction, 169, 207, 326

word problems, 199–202, 281

V

Vertical form. *See* Equations.

Visual thinking. *See* Spatial Reasoning.

W

What's the Error?, 18, 23, 60, 79, 84, 92, 93–94, 168, 176, 210, 231–232, 245, 248, 267–268, 326. *See also* Puzzled Penguin.

Word problems, 3, 5, 31–44, 49–60, 65–66, 77–78, 81, 90, 169, 182, 189–190, 195–196, 199–204, 207–209, 212, 213–214, 272, 275, 281, 285, 293–298, 315–317, 323–325. *See also* Problem Solving; Problem Types.

estimate answers, 196, 290

Z